C000196933

North Wales

Following Offa's Dyke Path towards Penycloddiau (Walk 24)

Best Walks in
North Wales

Twenty-eight of the finest circular walks in North Wales: covering the Isle of Anglesey, Lleyn Peninsula, northern Snowdonia and Northeast Wales

Carl Rogers

First published 2008 by

Northern Eye Books
Castleview, High Street,
Tattenhall,
Cheshire, CH3 9PX

www.northerneyebooks.com

ISBN 0 9553557 3 7
ISBN 978 0 9553557 3 8

For sales enquiries, please telephone: 01928 723744

Copyright © Carl Rogers 2008

Carl Rogers has asserted his right under the Copyright, Designs
and Patents Act, 1988 to be identified as the author of this work.
All rights reserved.

Maps and design by Carl Rogers.

Northern Eye Books Limited Reg. No. 05460709

A CIP catalogue record for this book is available from the British Library.

Whilst every effort has been made to ensure that the information in this book
is correct at the time of publication, neither the author nor the publisher can
accept any responsibility for any errors, loss or injury, however caused.

The routes described in this book are undertaken at the individual's own
risk. The publisher and copyright owners accept no responsibility for any
consequences arising from the use of this book, including misinterpretation
of the maps and directions.

Maps based on out of copyright Ordnance Survey mapping, aerial photographs and local
knowledge.

Printed and bound in Wales by Gomer Press, Ceredigion.

About the author

Carl Rogers has explored the hills, mountains and coastline of North Wales for over forty years making his first mountain ascent—Moel Siabod in Snowdonia—at the age of just six. Since then he has walked and climbed extensively in the Scottish Highlands and Cumbria, as well as the Alps and Norway.

After training as a graphic designer, he worked in marketing as a designer and photographer. In 2003 he became a self employed writer and publisher of outdoor literature through Mara Books and Northern Eye Books.

www.marabooks.co.uk

Acknowledgements

I would like to thank Lorna Jenner for the use of two walks from her book: *Walking in the Vale of Clwyd and Denbigh Moors* (walks 22 & 23). Thanks also to Jack Rogers, Audrey Rogers and Bob Nash for their help in revising and route-checking the walks in this book.

Contents

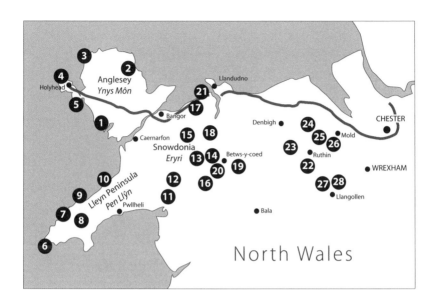

Northeast Wales

North Wales: *A Walker's Paradise*

HERE, GATHERED TOGETHER in one book, are some of the very best walks in North Wales. These carefully chosen and deliberately undemanding routes cover the finest and most spectacular parts of North Wales—from sea-girt Anglesey and Lleyn on the western fringe of North Wales, through the magnificent mountain scenery of central Snowdonia and the Conwy Valley, to the rolling hills of the Clwydian Range and the Vale of Llangollen in the east. Together, they will take you through some of the loveliest landscapes of this Celtic heartland—along rocky coasts with hidden bays, beside mountain streams and mirrored upland lakes, and over heather-clad hills whose panoramic views will delight the eye and enliven the senses.

For ease of use, the walks are arranged into four clear geographical sections: Anglesey; Lleyn Peninsula; Northern

The Snowdon Horseshoe from Llynnau Mymbyr, Capel Curig

The remains of a nineteenth century shipwreck on an Anglesey beach

Snowdonia and Northeast Wales. All are fairly low level, easy to moderate routes without serious or strenuous climbs or steep descents. They vary in length from 8-13 kilometres / 5-8½ miles, and many incorporate a short cut for those pressed for either time or energy. Each of the carefully planned circular walks features a useful overview and factfile at the beginning and a clear and accurate map, as well as handy details of the distance, parking, amenities, relevant Ordnance Survey maps and a grid reference for the starting point. Similarly, the walking directions are broken down into easy-to-follow numbered sections that correspond to numbers on the maps. Already tried and tested by many thousands of walkers, these are walks that work.

There is no need for any specialist equipment, beyond a pair of comfortable walking boots, relevant Ordnance Survey maps, and a day sack for waterproofs, food and drink, and perhaps sunscreen and a hat in summer. All of which mean you're free to relax and enjoy the day, confident of the route ahead.

Yr Wyddfa, the highest summit in Wales, under winter conditions

The best maps for walking are undoubtedly the Ordnance Survey's 1:25,000 Explorer and Outdoor Leisure series. Many are double sided, and all show the entire public rights of way network, as well as field boundaries, pubs, permissive paths and access land.

Remember, too, that the weather can change rapidly in the hills and mountains. Keep an eye out for weather reports at tourist information offices, outdoors centres and on local noticeboards. Or take a look at: www.mountainweatherwales.org before you set out.

North Wales is a dramatic landscape with something to stir the blood of walkers of every taste and ability. At its heart lies the huge and rugged Snowdonia National Park, embracing cloud-wrapped mountains, deep glacial valleys, tranquil lakes, soaring cliffs and plunging waterfalls—as well as forest, moorland and seashore. Snowdonia itself is home to Wales' fourteen highest peaks, all over 914 metres/3,000 feet, topped by Snowdon, whose highest summit, Yr Wyddfa, rises to 1085 metres/3,560 feet.

From Roman times onwards, this natural mountain fortress has protected the Welsh from invaders. Llywelyn, the last Prince of Wales, retreated here to lick his wounds in 1277; and later, Snowdonia was Owain Glyndŵr's last redoubt in his fight for an independent Wales. Centuries on, English slate barons made their fortunes here, on the backs of Welsh workers, in the mines and quarries; today, their dark spoil heaps and derelict works bring an atmospheric edge to the area's natural scenic grandeur.

From the mid-nineteenth century onwards, Snowdonia drew ever-increasing numbers of visitors to marvel at her mountains, lakes and waterfalls. Numbers have grown ever since. Today, thousands of enthusiasts converge on Snowdonia during holidays and at weekends to enjoy what, by consensus, is the most dramatic and alluring part of Wales.

Further west lie Ynys Môn, or Anglesey, and the Lleyn Peninsula. In contrast to the mountainous mainland, Anglesey is largely flat, levelled by successive ice sheets and subsequent

The Skerries off the northwest tip of Anglesey

Llantysilio Mountain rising above the Dee Valley

erosion. The resulting glacial boulder clays make for some of Wales' richest farmland; and the island was once known as *Mam Cymru*, or the 'mother of Wales' for her role as the country's bread basket. Away from the attractively varied coast, the landscape remains largely pastoral, with small fields, drystone walls, and traditional white-painted stone houses.

The Lleyn takes its name from an old Irish word for 'peninsula'. Known sometimes as the 'Land's End of Wales', it's a still relatively unknown, rocky finger jutting south-west into the Irish Sea. With its tiny coves and sandy bays, the wild north coast, especially, is a walkers' paradise. From the distinctive triple peaks of Yr Eifl, the hills diminish towards Aberdaron, at the tip of the Lleyn—from where early pilgrims once set sail for Ynys Enlli, or Bardsey, the remote 'island of 20,000 saints'.

Away to the east, closer to England, are the Borderlands: the green and rounded Clwydian Range, the pretty Vale of Llangollen, and the open heaths and forests of the Denbigh Moors. Quite rightly, the Clwydian Range is a designated Area of Outstanding Natural Beauty (AONB) and one of only eight protected landscapes in Wales. Stretching for 22 miles/35 kilometres from north to south, the heather-clad hills are punctuated by limestone outcrops and wooded escarpments. The northern section of the long distance Offa's Dyke National Trail hugs the ridge, and there are popular country parks at Loggerheads and Moel Famau.

A stone's throw away, the picturesque Vale of Llangollen follows the River Dee as it cuts through the hills. This ancient strategic route is guarded by ruined Castell Dinas Bran on its conical hill above Llangollen. Centred on a four-arched medieval bridge, the tiny town of Llangollen is probably best known for the Llangollen International Musical Eisteddfod, which it hosts every year in July.

Less visited are the open heather and sheepwalks of the Denbigh Moors, including the vast Clocaenog Forest and the

Alwen and Brenig reservoirs. Together, these varied landscapes offer breathtaking views, abundant wildlife and superb walking. There really is something for everyone.

The walks in this book have been selected from a range of walking books covering the whole of North Wales and published by Mara Books, a sister imprint of Northern Eye Books. All are currently in print and may be purchased separately by those who want to explore further routes in a particular favourite area. Titles include: *Coastal Walks around Anglesey*; *Walks on the Lleyn Peninsula*; *Walking in Snowdonia Volume 1*; *Walking in the Conwy Valley*; *Walking in the Clwydian Range*; and *Walking in the Vale of Clwyd and Denbigh Moors*. For details of the complete catalogue, prices, and how to order visit our website: www.northerneyebooks.com.

Happy walking.

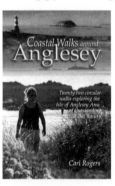
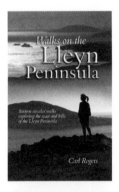
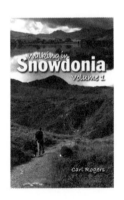
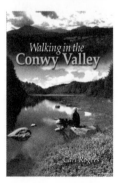
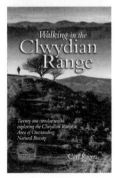

Isle of Anglesey
Ynys Môn

1. Aberffraw & Porth Cwyfan

Along the low, rocky shore to a curious island church

A lovely section of the Anglesey coastal path with broad views across Caernarfon Bay to the hills of the Lleyn Peninsula

Start: *Begin the walk in the village of Aberffraw. There is free parking available for a number of cars on common land beside the old bridge. Map reference: SH 356 689.*

Distance: *8 kilometres/5 miles.*

Duration: *Allow 2-3 hours.*

Difficulty: *Easy. An almost level coastal walk with a return across farmland and quiet lanes. Excellent footpaths throughout.*

Food and Drink: *Y Goron (The Crown), Bodorgan Square, Aberffraw. 01407 840397.*

Map: *OS 1: 50,000 Landranger 114 Anglesey; OS 1:25,000 Explorer 262 Anglesey West.*

SEA VIEWS TO THE LLEYN AND SNOWDONIA enliven this low-level coastal walk. Across the shallow clear waters of Caernarfon Bay, the shapely hills of the Lleyn Peninsula line the horizon, while the higher peaks of Snowdonia peep over the headland at the end of the bay.

The walk

1. Cross the old bridge and turn left immediately onto a track which runs beside the river. Where the track bears left onto the sand, continue along the shore to the river mouth.

(If the water is high or the shore too wet, turn right onto a narrow signed footpath, then turn left between gardens. This path takes you back to the shore where a low wall runs above the sand. Follow the path along the top of the wall, then drop onto the sand just before a white cottage and continue to the river mouth.)

Originally, Aberffraw was open to the sea and even enjoyed a brief period of prosperity as a small port. Over the centuries however, the estuary on which it lies has become filled with wind-blown sand with the result that today over half-a-mile of sand dunes separate it from the sea. In its original state, the estuary would have been something like the nearby Malltraeth Sands and extended inland for over two miles. Llyn Coron, near Bodorgan Station, which is now a freshwater lake, marks the original limit of the estuary.

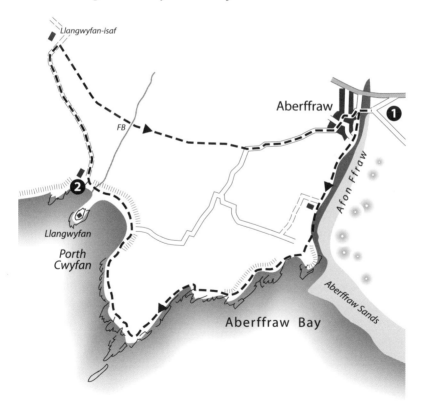

Today, you will find nothing at Aberffraw to suggest its past importance as the administrative centre for the kings and princes of the kingdom of Gwynedd, which covered much of North Wales. For eight hundred years, Welsh kings and princes used the royal palace here as a base in their fight against invasions from the Irish, Saxons, Vikings and finally Normans.

The palace was established by a British chieftain called Cunedda, who came from Strathclyde with his sons and a large army of fighting men, to rid North Wales of Irish tribes who had attacked and overrun the kingdom, following the Roman withdrawal. Cunedda was able to pass on to his sons a vast kingdom that encompassed much of present day North Wales. His grandson, Cadwallon, who inherited the northern kingdom that would become Gwynedd, is credited with finally ridding Wales of the Irish in a last battle on Anglesey about AD 470. Other rulers associated with Aberffraw include Cadwallon's son, Maelgwyn Gwynedd, who granted land for the founding of monasteries at Holyhead and Penmon in the mid sixth century and Rhodri Mawr (Rhodri the Great 844-878), who ruled much of Wales from his seat at Aberffraw, as did Llywelyn the Great. Other prominent names include Gruffydd ap Cynan, who died in 1137 at the remarkable age of 82, his son Owain Gwynedd and Llywelyn 'the Last', whose defeat by Edward I in 1282 brought Welsh independence to an end.

With such a long period of use—something like the period that separates our own time from that of Edward I—it is perhaps surprising that no trace of the palace is now to be seen. The reason for this is that throughout its long history it was built entirely from wood, a fact which made possible its partial destruction by the Vikings in 968. The building of castles and churches from stone did not really begin until after the Norman conquest and even then, the earliest motte and bailey castles were usually of timber construction. Although this may seem strange as we look at the bare treeless landscape of today, for much of the period that the palace was in use, Anglesey was thickly wooded. By the fourteenth century, timber was evidently in shorter supply, for we are told that in 1317 the palace was demolished and its timbers used to repair Caernarfon Castle.

The tiny Celtic church of Saint Cwyfan

Just before the mouth of the river, bear right through a kissing gate onto the coastal footpath. Before you do this, walk left across the grass to the end of the little promontory for a fine view of the bay.

This is one of the most beautiful bays in Wales and is perhaps seen at its best on a clear summer evening when the crowds have left the beach. Across the water are the blue outlines of Gryn Ddu, Yr Eifl and distant hills of Lleyn.

The coastal path (to the right) from here is easy to follow and keeps to the edge of the low rocks with occasional departures into small coves and onto wave-cut rocks. Ignore signed footpaths on the right which lead inland. Keep your eyes open for grey seals, which can frequently be seen in these shallow waters. Continue to Porth Cwyfan, a wide bay with a tiny church on a small island. A short walk along the shingle beach takes you onto the island, which is cut off at high tide.

This tiny isolated church dedicated to Saint Cwyfan was founded in the seventh century and rebuilt in stone during the twelfth century. In the centuries that followed, it was added to a number of times before being fully restored in the nineteenth century. Despite this, it has managed to retain its original simple form. The stone wall which surrounds the island was built during the nineteenth century restoration to counteract severe erosion problems. Outside the church a few scattered gravestones remain from the eighteenth century, along with a memorial to Frank Morley, a youngster of 20 who drowned in nearby Porth Trecastell.

2. Continue along the beach past the church. At the far end of the bay an access track reaches down onto the beach beside a small cottage (don't confuse this with a lane passed earlier *before* the church). Walk up the track passing the Anglesey Racing Circuit on your left.

Look for a signed footpath on your right just before a large house (Llangwyfan-isaf) in wooded gardens on the left. Go through the kissing gate and walk ahead through the centre of a large open field to cross a stile. Continue ahead in the following field to a kissing gate and footbridge over a stream. Cross the footbridge and follow the right of way ahead along the left-hand field edge to cross a farm track almost in the top corner of the field. Go through a kissing gate here and bear half-left through the field to a footbridge over a ditch. Head half-left again across the following field to steps near an old kissing gate. Go ahead along the field edge to a lane.

Turn left along the lane and walk back to Aberffraw. In the centre of the village by the post office, turn right. Pass 'Y Goron' ('The Crown') pub and continue down to cross the old bridge to complete the walk.

2. Traeth yr Ora & Mynydd Bodafon

Beach, estuary and hilltop panorama

One of Anglesey's finest beaches, a secluded estuary, and the breezy viewpoint at Mynydd Bodafon

Start: *Begin the walk at the beach car park at Traeth Lligwy. This lies at the end of a narrow lane running northwest from the A5025 at Brynrefail, between Moelfre and Amlwch, on Anglesey. Map reference: SH 492 873.*

Distance: *6 or 10 kilometres/3¾ or 6½ miles.*

Duration: *Allow 3-3½ hours.*

Difficulty: *Moderate. Some steep ascents to Mynydd Bodafon.*

Food and Drink: *Pilot Boat Inn, Dulas. Real ale. Good food. Children welcome. 01248 410205.*

Map: *OS 1: 50,000 Landranger 114 Anglesey; OS 1:25,000 Explorer 263 Anglesey East.*

CONTRASTING VIEWPOINTS add an unusual dimension to this circuit. Centered on one of the most attractive beaches on this side of Anglesey, the walk then ascends to take in the breezy panoramas from the modest summit of Mynydd Bodafon.

The walk

1. From the car park follow the signed coastal path to the left (when facing the sea) which runs north to the small sand and shingle beach of Porth-y-Môr (1 kilometre / ¾ mile).

Immediately ahead you can see the rocks of Ynys Dulas, which lie a mile or so offshore. The tower was built in 1824 as a beacon to identify the treacherous reef, of which the island is only a small part. The tower incorporated a refuge and was stocked with food and provisions.

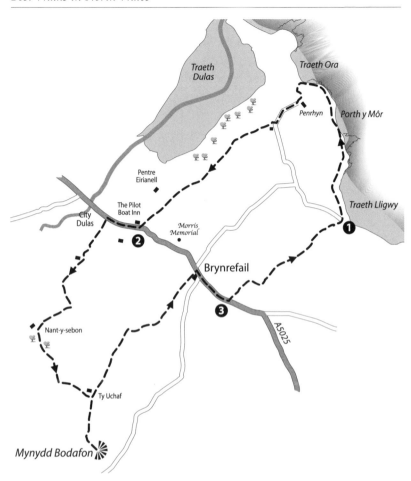

Walk ahead along the beach (ignore a stile on the left) and then continue on the obvious coastal path to Traeth Ora, a beautifully secluded sandy cove which cannot be approached by road. There is a kissing gate, a bench and a waymarker post immediately above the beach here.

(A footpath leads ahead through the bracken to the far end of the bay and the little headland which encloses the tidal eastuary of Traeth Dulas. It is a beautifully secluded spot and is well worth a visit, but you must return to this point to continue the walk.)

To continue, turn left on the well worn footpath (right if you took the detour to the end of the bay), which rises to Penrhyn Farm. Turn right at the farm onto the access track which eventually joins a tarmac road. Continue straight ahead up the lane and immediately before the first bend turn right onto a signed footpath around the garden of a cottage to enter fields through a kissing gate on the left.

Walk ahead up the gently sloping field with the sands and marshes of Traeth Dulas down to the right. Near the top of the field look for a squat waymarker post on the left, which directs you half-left through a gap in the hedge. At the time of writing there is a fenced enclosure on the other side of the hedge. Go ahead to the right of the fence to the corner by an overgrown wall, then turn right between the fence and wall. At the end of the fence keep along the left-hand side of the field to cross a ladder

Traeth Lligwy

stile. Continue ahead (diverting around a pond if neccessary), to a gate and ladder stile in the far left corner leading onto a farm track. Follow the track for about 300 metres, and where this bears right, go through a kissing gate directly ahead into fields once more. Walk ahead along the right-hand field edge to the 'Pilot Boat Inn'.

2. Turn right down the hill passing the signed coastal footpath on the right. Just after the 'City Dulas' sign and before houses, take the signed footpath on the left. Follow the right of way along the left-hand field edge with Mynydd Bodafon directly ahead. At an access track turn right and follow it towards a bungalow. Go through a small gate on the left immediately before the bungalow and follow a path around the garden to a footbridge and stile into fields. Turn right and walk along the field edge to a stile and ahead again in the following field beside the stream.

At a shallow ditch separating two fields turn left and walk beside it. At the top of the field turn right over a footbridge then immediately left over a stile. Go right now on a good path to a footpath junction with ruins on the right.

Go ahead here over a stile, cross a footbridge over the stream and turn left immediately up the bank with the stream on your left. Higher up, bear right to cross a ladder stile on the left. Go ahead along the left-hand edge of the following fields to a ladder stile on the left in a field corner. Cross the stile and walk beside the right-hand fence in the following fields to a farm. Immediately before the outbuildings, go through a gate on the right and follow the track as it curves left to a junction of tracks by 'Ty Uchaf'.

Turn right here and follow the obvious footpath that heads directly across the open heather-covered hillside heading directly for the triangulation pillar on the summit of Mynydd Bodafon. As you approach the top, bear left to the summit.

Although it rises to a modest 178 metres/584 feet, this little hill gives a fine panorama over Anglesey's predominantly flat landscape. Out to the west you can see Holyhead Mountain and Mynydd y Garn along

Mynydd Bodafon

with the collection of wind farms near Cemaes Bay. Nearer at hand you have the spoil heaps of Parys Mountain, where copper has been mined since prehistoric times, and Mynydd Eilian with its two masts. Out to the east you will be able to see Puffin Island near Penmon Head, along with the wide mouth of Red Wharf Bay and the blunt headland of the Great Orme near Llandudno on the horizon.

To the south, the interior of the island is rather featureless although the basic structure—a series of shallow valleys running northeast to southwest—can plainly be seen. It is one of these valleys which, now flooded, forms the Menai Strait separating Anglesey from the mainland. A second valley running between Malltraeth and Red Wharf Bay almost divides the island in two, although much of it has now been reclaimed.

Back towards the mainland, the peaks of Snowdonia fill the southern skyline: from the rounded whaleback slopes of the Carneddau in the east, to the sculptured pinnacles of Tryfan and Crib Goch on Snowdon. Farther west, the isolated hills of the Lleyn Peninsula stand plainly on the farthest skyline.

Retrace you steps back to the junction of tracks at 'Ty Uchaf' and take the track directly ahead. Pass cottages on the left and go over the stile by the gate to 'Cae'r Mynydd' directly ahead. Walk through the garden to steps into fields again. Walk ahead to a stile in the corner of the first field then ahead through a large field to stiles and a footbridge. Keep ahead again to a stile into a rough area of gorse. A good path leads ahead through the gorse to a stile over the wall by rocks on the right. Keep to the right-hand edge of the fields and about 100 metres after the fence on the right ends, turn left across the field to pass beside a narrow woodland on the left. Drop down the bank and go through a kissing gate on the left. Turn right along the fenced wall to the corner of the field and climb steps over the wall near a bungalow on the right. Walk through a small field to a gate into the lane and turn left to Brynrefail. Turn right at the A5025.

3. After about 500 metres look for a signed footpath on the left that leads into fields. Go through the gate and ahead along field edges. Ignore a signed 'Permissive Path', keeping straight ahead and in the following field, immediately before a large house, turn right though a kissing gate. Follow the path beside the garden to a kissing gate in the bottom corner on the left. Go through the gate onto a drive beside the gateway to 'Siop y Rhos' and turn right down the drive. Almost immediately, where this turns right, go left over a stile and ahead along the edge of the field to cross a second stile. Follow a footpath between hedges now, to a farm on the right. Go ahead through a large narrow field to a stile in the far hedgeline. This leads onto a path through gorse hedges to join a track. Turn left and follow the track back to the beach car park to complete the walk.

3. Cemlyn Bay to Carmel Head

Anglesey's remote northwest corner

Gentle clifftop walking with views out to the famous Skerries

Start: *Begin the walk at a small, free National Trust car park near Trwyn Cemlyn. This is approached by following the lane to Cemlyn Bay but instead of turning right down the short lane which leads to the bay, take the next right. After about 400 metres turn right down to Trwyn Cemlyn.*
Map reference: SH 329 935.

Distance: *10.5 kilometres/6½ miles.*

Duration: *Allow 3-3½ miles.*

Difficulty: *Easy. Footpaths are a little indistinct in places.*

Food and Drink: *No refreshments on the route or nearby.*

Map: *OS 1: 50,000 Landranger 114 Anglesey; OS 1:25,000 Explorer 262 Anglesey West.*

FROM THE SHELTER OF CEMLYN BAY to the wild, weather-beaten rocks along the coast towards Carmel Head, this is a walk full of drama and contrast.

The walk

1. From the car park walk along the gravel track which leads onto the National Trust land at Trwyn Cemlyn.

On the way, there is a stone memorial on the right to commemorate the 150th anniversary of the first lifeboat on Anglesey (1828-1978). This was founded by the Reverend James Williams and his wife Frances after witnessing the wreck of the Irish Packet 'Alert' which drifted onto West Mouse killing 145 people in 1823. The Reverend and his wife are

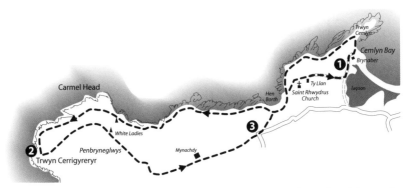

said to have watched helplessly from this headland as the ship sank, leaving only seven survivors.

James and Frances devoted the rest of their lives to the formation of the Anglesey Association for the Preservation of Life from Shipwreck. James was awarded the first RNLI Gold Medal in Wales, after playing a major role in the rescue of sailors from the vessel 'Active', wrecked in Cemaes Bay in 1835. Ironically, it was not at the helm of his lifeboat but from the shore, where he used his horse to get deeper into the surf and throw a grappling iron to the wreck, thus saving the lives of five men.

Here you can either walk over rough grass to the end of the headland for a view of the bay, or bear left following the wall to a corner overlooking the rocky shore, where a kissing gate leads into fields on your left. The path now keeps tight against the right-hand field boundary, overlooking the sea to your right.

At low tide there is a panorama of wave-cut rocks and small islands out towards The Skerries. On a blustery day, there is a strong Hebridean feel to this remote weather-beaten corner of Anglesey, which stands in sharp contrast to the softer south and east coasts.

These notorious reefs have been a hazard to shipping for centuries and caused the wreck, in 1854, of the steamer 'Olinda' which hit Harry Furlough's Rocks and broke up. Fortunately, all those on board were rescued by the Cemlyn Lifeboat.

Continue along the coastal footpath passing above Ty'n Llan farm and the little church of Saint Rhwydrus which can be seen down to the left, to the next cove (Hen Borth) a small shingle bay.

Continue along the coastal path which hugs the edge of fields almost to Carmel Head where you will see the curious stone structures known as the 'White Ladies'—almost 4 kilometres/ 2 miles.

This wild treacherous coastline overlooks the busy shipping lane to Liverpool and has been a major hazard for centuries. Sailing ships were particularly vulnerable and were frequently driven onto its notorious reefs and islands by onshore winds.

Northwest of Carmel Head lies the group of rocks known as The Skerries—a Norse name derived from the word 'sker' meaning 'steep rock'. In Welsh they are known as Ynysoedd y Moelrhoniaid or 'Seal Islands' and were the scene in 1675 of the wreck of Britain's first Royal Yacht, the 'Mary' presented to Charles II. The remains of this ship were found by accident in 1971 in 12 metres of water.

Originally, The Skerries were owned by Bangor Cathedral but were diverted into private ownership by Bishop Nicholas Robinson during the 1570s. In 1713, the islands were leased by a descendant of the Bishop's to William Tench. He built the first beacon in 1716 and planned to collect duties from shipping entering Holyhead, however, the venture proved to be disastrous and he died penniless in 1725. Tragically, he also lost

Following the coastal path near Cemlyn Bay

The Skerries

his son who drowned while ferrying coal to The Skerries to keep the beacon running. Another tragedy happened to a descendant of Bishop Robinson on the 20th June 1739, when William Robinson and twelve companions drowned while returning from the beacon. Their empty boat was washed ashore four days later at Whitehaven in Cumbria.

After a long and troubled history The Skerries became the last privately owned lighthouse in the country and was eventually sold for £444,984 11s 2d in 1841.

A rather curious wreck occurred at Carmel Head in the early 1740s, when an unknown vessel sank leaving two young boys as the only survivors. They came ashore lashed to a raft but as they could speak no Welsh or English, they could tell their rescuers nothing about the ship or its crew. One of the boys was adopted by a local family and given the name Evan Thomas. Evan eventually learned to speak Welsh and found that he had a gift for setting bones, which he later developed into a successful business. His descendants founded the Robert Jones and Agnes Hunt Orthopaedic Hospital near Oswestry. Nothing is recorded about the second youngster but both boys are assumed to have been Spanish.

Other links with shipping can be seen nearby in the form of the two large beacons known as the 'White Ladies'. These line up with a similar tower on West Mouse, to act as a guide for shipping negotiating Carmel Head.

Near the White Ladies, the coastal path leaves the rocky coastal edge, which swings rightwards to Carmel Head. The coastal path goes ahead and slightly left, indicated by waymarker posts, to cross a footbridge over a ditch. Keep ahead passing a tall chimney associated with local mining, and continue until Holyhead Mountain comes into view and you are forced to rise leftwards to a prominent rocky summit above the headland of Trwyn Cerrigyreryr.

From here there is a wide view of Holyhead Bay. To the southwest you will see the Irish ferries arriving and leaving Holyhead Harbour as they have done for centuries. Behind the town, Holyhead Mountain rises to over 245 metres, the highest point on the island. Further south, the chimney at the aluminium works forms a prominent and well known landmark. On clear days, or just before sunset, you can often see the hills of southern Ireland on the western horizon. To the south, the coast becomes less dramatic beyond Church Bay, although the coves between Carmel Head and Porth y Bribys present some of the grandest sea cliff scenery on the island.

The wide panorama from this hilltop was first exploited by the Romans, who are thought to have built a beacon and lookout on the summit of nearby Penbrynyreglwys, to guard the entrance to their harbour at what is now Holyhead.

2. Head back towards the mine ruins (chimney) seen earlier. These are not visible yet and there are few trails to follow, so cut across the open hillside aiming just to the right of the beacon on West Mouse but keeping to the left of the rounded flat summit of Penbrynyreglwys, until the ruins come into view. The chimney is the first to be seen along with a view east along the north coast.

The mines date from a period of prosperity in the copper industry during the eighteenth century, although there is evidence of mining here in prehistoric times.

Pass between the ruins on your left and the chimney on the right and pick up a grass track which contours the hillside to a gate beyond the White Ladies beacons. Beyond the gate, follow the track through a larger grazing field to a gate and stone steps in the far corner. Bear half-right through a smaller field to a ladder stile about 150 metres away and head left along a track that soon curves to the right around a small artificial pool backed by conifer woods. Follow the track towards farm buildings at Mynachdy and pass through the farmyard to a gate immediately ahead. Go through the gate and follow the obvious track through grazing fields to a lane.

3. Walk ahead a few paces and immediately before a small National Trust car park turn left through a kissing gate. Cross a footbridge and follow the footpath beside a stream. Go through a second kissing gate and keep ahead to join the coastal path again at the small bay of Hen Borth. Turn right and at the end of the shingle beach go through the kissing gate into fields. Keep along the field edge and after the next kissing gate bear half-right across the field to the little church of Saint Rhwydrus.

Dedicated to Saint Rhwydrus, the simple form and plain interior of the church are typical of many small Celtic churches on Anglesey. The font and nave date from the twelfth century and the chancel dates from a century later. In the little cemetery surrounding the church there are a number of graves from the eighteenth and nineteenth centuries, with at least one dated 1676.

Pass to the left of the church and cemetery (where steps lead over the wall to visit the church) and walk towards the farmhouse directly ahead. Enter the farmyard and go ahead down the access road. At the end of the road turn left and return to the car park to complete the walk.

Approaching Porth Cwyfan, Anglesey (Walk 1)

Isle of Anglesey Coastal Path near Cemlyn Bay (Walk 3)

Ellin's Tower near South Stack, Anglesey (Walk 4)

Mynydd Mawr, Bardsey Island and the fields of Uwchmynydd, Lleyn (Walk 6)

Looking across Bardsey Sound to Bardsey Island, Lleyn (Walk 6)

The Snowdon Horseshoe from Llynnau Mymbyr, Capel Curig, Snowdonia (Walk 13)

Llyn Gwynant and Yr Aran, Snowdonia (Walk 12)

Llyn Idwal and the Devil's Kitchen, Snowdonia (Walk 15)

Castell Dolwyddelan, Snowdonia (Walk 16)

The Llugwy valley, Betws-y-Coed, Snowdonia (Walk 14)

The rolling hills above the village of Cyfflliog, Denbighshire (Walk 22)

Moel Famau from the Vale of Clwyd, Denbighshire (Walk 25)

Nantclwyd Hall, near Ruthin, Denbighshire (Walk 26)

The Dee Valley from Llantysilio Mountain, Denbighshire (Walk 27)

Castell Dinas Bran, Denbighshire (Walk 28)

4. Holyhead Mountain
Above the cliffs to the lighthouse

North Wales' highest sea cliffs, North Stack, South Stack lighthouse, and breathtaking sea views

---

Start: *Begin the walk at the 'Breakwater Country Park' in Holyhead, located at the northwestern end of the seafront, at the end of 'Beach Road'. Start from the little visitor centre. Map reference: SH 226 833.*

Distance: *8 kilometres /5 miles.*

Duration: *Allow 2½-3 hours.*

Difficulty: *Easy. Footpaths are good throughout.*

Food and Drink: *Café down the lane near Ellin's Tower.*

Map: *OS 1: 50,000 Landranger 114 Anglesey; OS 1:25,000 Explorer 262 Anglesey West.*

OPEN, BARE AND BREEZY, Holyhead Mountain promises spectacular walking with dramatic cliff scenery and striking views from Anglesey's highest point.

The walk

1. Cross the car park to pass through a gap in the wall and walk ahead along a gravel path passing a pool on the right. Go through a kissing gate onto a track and turn left. In about 50 metres bear right through a kissing gate beside a field gate. The path goes ahead through rough grass and gorse towards a large quarry face. As you approach the cliff face the path curves right to a point overlooking the sea with a wide view back to Holyhead harbour. Bear left here onto a pitched path which contours the slopes. Stay on the stone-pitched path ignoring minor paths here and there and soon you will be able to see along the coast to North Stack.

Pass the little squat stone building (keeping it below you) and continue up the steep pitched path. At a path junction bear right and follow the path down to North Stack.

As you approach the house at North Stack a track comes in sharply from the left, which you will use to continue the walk.

Anyone with a head for heights can walk down to the end of the rocks to the left of the boundary wall for an impressive view of the cliff scenery. Looking back you will see the enormous cavern beneath the house which will eventually separate the rock you are now standing on from the main cliff to create another stack. To the right there is a view along Gogarth Bay where there are a number of difficult rock climbs. Climbers can often be seen on the face.

2. Walk back to the house and turn right up the track until it begins to level and there is a junction of paths. Take the signed coastal path which bears right here. This has been stone pitched

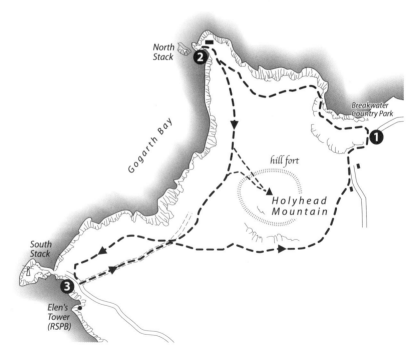

Looking across Gogarth Bay to South Stack Lighthouse

and rises in a series of steps up towards Holyhead Mountain. Ignore minor paths on the right as you rise, as these are paths mainly used by rock climbers to reach the cliffs below

Over to the right there is a superb view across Gogarth Bay towards South Stack.

Continue until the path levels with Holyhead Mountain ahead. Make a slight drop to a broad saddle. (A left fork here will take you to the summit of Holyhead Mountain. If you take the summit detour return to the saddle to continue the walk.) Keep ahead on the coastal path which will take you over the shoulder of the mountain towards South Stack.

Soon communication dishes come into view. Keep ahead and, immediately adjacent to the dishes (on the right), bear right off the main path onto a narrower path which leads to the tarmac access road to the dishes. Turn left along the road for about 30 metres then bear right onto a stony footpath passing close to brick buildings on the left beneath a radio mast. This path bends right, drops slightly, then rises to pass along a rounded heather ridge with a small pool down to the left. Soon you will find yourself in a dramatic position overlooking South Stack Lighthouse from beside the ruins of the old telegraph station. Head half-left from here to reach the road head directly above the lighthouse.

South Stack is one of the most spectacular locations on Anglesey and its lighthouse is probably one of the most photographed in Wales. Construction of a beacon here began in 1798 and cost over £12,000. The structure was finished and its oil lamp first lit on 9 February 1809. The present structure was automated in 1984 when the keepers were withdrawn. Today it is monitored by computer link from the Trinity House Operations Centre in Harwich, Essex.

3. Turn left along the road for about 100 metres or so and turn left up a signed tarmac/concrete road. At a crossing track take the path ahead and at a fork keep ahead again, soon passing the brick buildings passed earlier. At the next junction (below the 'dishes' again), bear right. This path takes you close below the crags of Holyhead Mountain, then bears right. Keep left at a fork and rise slightly onto the rocky shoulder of the mountain, ignoring a track on the right that leads to a small quarry. At the next junction keep ahead contouring past small wall-enclosed fields on the right.

As Holyhead comes into view, the path enters walled enclosures. Where two paths cross, keep ahead. Soon there is a wide view of the breakwater reaching out into the bay. At a junction of access roads turn left and left again at a T junction. At the road end bear left along a grass path (adjacent to a house 'Cornish'). At a fork in 50 metres or so, turn right, soon passing beside a wire-link fence on the left. At a T junction turn left down steps, then left again to return to the Breakwater Country Park to complete the walk.

5. Penrhyn Mawr
Heather and headlands

Over flower-rich lowland heath to a series of headlands and coves, with wide views to South Stack and beyond

Start: *There is free parking at Penrhyn Mawr, a large open heather covered headland accessed from a short lane between Trearddur and South Stack. Map reference: SH 216 803.*

Distance: *13 kilometres/8¼ miles.*

Duration: *Allow 3-4 hours.*

Difficulty: *Easy. Mainly level walking on level footpaths.*

Food and Drink: *No refreshments on the route.*

Map: *OS 1: 50,000 Landranger 114 Anglesey; OS 1:25,000 Explorer 262 Anglesey West.*

PURPLE HEATHER, YELLOW GORSE, tiny coves and distant views out to sea characterise this attractive coastal circuit.

The walk

1. At the back of the car park there is a fingerpost indicating the coastal path both to the left and right. Take the right-hand option heading in the direction of South Stack Lighthouse. At a crossing path turn left. At the coast bear left onto the coastal path. Pass round the back of Porth Ruffydd and keep following the coast, bearing inland slightly at the rocky head of Dinas to go through a kissing gate. Walk round the grassy headland, passing through another gate to join a narrow path heading towards a caravan park. Join the path to Porth Dafarch beach. Cross the little cove and bear right onto the signed coastal path again.

Walk around the headland and as you approach a house cross a wooden footbridge and stile and walk along an enclosed path to join the drive to a house on the right. Turn left up the drive to the road. Turn right and walk along the road for approximately 500 metres.

2. Turn left down the access road to 'Isallt Fawr'. Pass houses on the left and at the end of the drive a footpath continues ahead to a ladder stile into fields. Cross the stile and walk along the right-hand field edges to an access road with houses on the right. Turn right here and walk along the access road to a T junction with a tarmac lane. Turn left along the lane and after about 100 metres take the signed field path on the right. Follow the path, which is enclosed at first, to enter a large field. Bear right through the field to a kissing gate in the far corner near bungalows. Go ahead to join an estate road and turn left.

At a T junction at the end of the road, turn left again and look for a signed footpath on the right. Turn right over the ladder stile and walk around the right-hand field edge. At a stile on the right,

Looking north from Penrhyn Mawr to South Stack Lighthouse

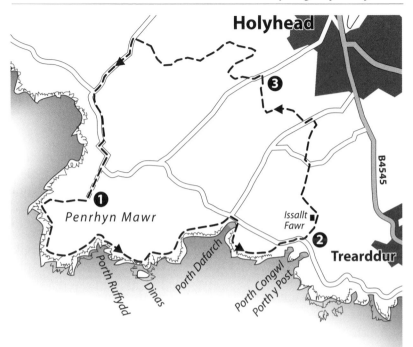

cross over and walk ahead to a ladder stile by a gate. Cross the stile and follow the well worn footpath through an area of rocks and gorse. Keep to the most obvious footpath (marked by the 'St Cybi Circular Walk' symbol, although many of the waymarkers are missing at the time of writing) ignoring minor footpaths on either side. Where Holyhead Mountain comes into view with a bungalow a field or so ahead, bear right over flat rocks—initially in the direction of a distant church tower in Holyhead. Don't go into smaller fields on the right, keep ahead between gorse bushes until you reach a bungalow beyond a fence. Bear left along the fence in front of the bungalow to a gate into a lane.

3. Turn left up the lane to a stile and sign on the right. Go over the stile and walk ahead to a gap in the wall/hedge, then ahead again with Holyhead Mountain ahead to a stile in an area of gorse. Cross the stile and continue through the area of gorse and flat rocks on a visible footpath.

At a wall and kissing gate, don't go through the gate, instead turn left to a stile in the corner. Go over this stile and follow the path ahead with a wall on the right. Pass a farmhouse on the right continuing ahead. Soon the footpath bears left to pass below some small rock outcrops on the left. After the outcrops go through a kissing gate on the right and keep ahead on a good footpath with Holyhead Mountain ahead again. In the field corner bear left with the fence.

Near a farm on the right, continue ahead to a waymarked gap in the fence on the right. Go through the gap and keep ahead with Holyhead Mountain ahead again and a farm on the right. Soon a waymarker post directs you right to a ladder stile. Go over the stile then bear left through a small field past a gorse covered bank on the right. Walk ahead to a gateway with an overhead power cable post beside it. Go through the gate and follow a path up the following field towards a farm. Walk ahead between the outbuildings (but to the left of the farmhouse) to a gate into a road.

Turn left along the road for about 1 kilometre / ¾ mile.

Opposite a lane on the right (this is the first lane you will meet and leads to South Stack), turn left up the bank onto a new permissive footpath (signed for the coastal path), which runs parallel to the road. At the end of the path join the road for about 400 metres before turning right down the access road to Penrhyn Mawr to complete the walk

Lleyn Peninsula
Pen Llŷn

6. Uwchmynydd
Around the rocky tip of Lleyn

A fine coastal walk around the 'Land's End of Lleyn' with breezy sea views out to Bardsey Island

Start: *Begin the walk in Aberdaron where there is a large pay and display car park and toilet facilities by the old bridge. Map reference: SH 173 264. An alternative start can be made from the free car park below Mynydd Mawr (Point 2), situated at the end of the narrow lane leading southwest from Aberdaron.*
Map reference: SH 142 255. This option omits the section between Aberdaron and Porth Meudwy.

Distance: *6.5 kilometres/4½ miles.*

Duration: *Allow 2½-3 hours.*

Difficulty: *Footpaths are excellent throughout using well maintained coastal path, quiet lanes and field paths.*

Food and Drink: *Several pubs and cafés in Aberdaron. Gwesty Ship Hotel, Aberdaron. Food and accommodation. 01758 760204. Tŷ Newydd, Aberdaron. Food and accommodation. 01758 760207.*

Map: *OS 1: 50,000 Landranger 123 Lleyn Peninsula; OS 1:25,000 Explorer 253 Lleyn Peninsula West.*

FLAT, TREELESS AND FRACTURED BY DRYSTONE WALLS, the uttermost tip of Lleyn is a land apart. But it is the westward-looking views out to Bardsey/Ynys Enlli that make this coastal walk so memorable.

The walk

1. Turn right out the car park, cross the old bridge and pass between buildings ahead to the beach. Turn right along the sand.

Aberdaron is the most westerly village in Lleyn and was traditionally

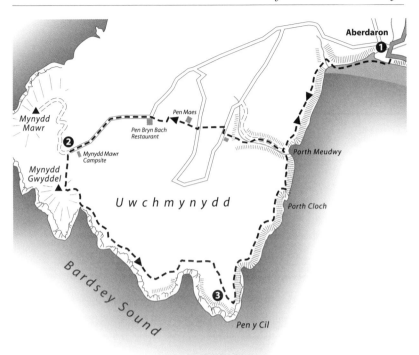

the end of the 'Saint's Road' taken by pilgrims en-route to Bardsey during the Middle Ages. Three pilgrimages to Bardsey were said to equal one to Rome.

Unfortunately, Aberdaron did not mark the end of their labours, the most hazardous part of the journey, albeit a short one, was yet to come — the crossing of Bardsey Sound. This has proved to be one of the most treacherous stretches of water around the Welsh coast — powerful tide races and hidden rocks can prove fatal even to modern engine driven craft — to the primitive sailing boats of the Dark Ages it must have been a major undertaking. Pilgrims often had to wait several days for favourable conditions both to reach and leave the island.

During this period, Aberdaron had many notable visitors, among them Gruffydd ap Cynan, the future prince of Gwynedd, who was given sanctuary after his escape from Chester Castle and Rhys of Deheubarth, who was in hiding from both Gruffydd ap Cynan and Henry I.

Aberdaron church

Probably the most unusual and colourful character to be associated with Aberdaron was Richard Robert Jones or 'Dic Aberdaron', who was born on a farm between Aberdaron and Porth Oer in 1780. Although his parents were probably illiterate, he reputedly learned to speak fluently and write in over fourteen languages. His love of foreign tongues and books took him on travels all over the country and his bizarre appearance, dress and unusual talent has turned him into a folklore figure. He died in 1843 at the age of 63 and is buried at St. Asaph church.

Ford the shallow river and at the far end of the bay go through the kissing gate and climb steps up to the clifftop coastal path. Turn left and follow the path to Porth Meudwy where steps lead down into the little cove.

Porth Meudwy or 'Port of the Hermit' was one of the embarkation points for pilgrims en-route to Bardsey, being the nearest safe anchorage to the island. Today there are no pilgrims or hermits, just a collection of fishing boats and lobster pots, but you can still take a boat to Bardsey from here.

Turn inland from here following a track up the little valley between high, bracken covered banks. Just before the track bears right and begins to rise, bear left on a narrow footpath to cross a footbridge and rise steeply to a small farm and campsite. Go ahead through the site to a lane. Turn right along the lane and after about 100 metres take the signed footpath on the left between fields. At a second lane turn right, then left almost immediately following the track to a stone cottage ('Pen Maes').

Bear left through a kissing gate just before the cottage and go up the right-hand side of the field to a stile in the corner. Cut directly across the next two fields aiming for an old grey farmhouse. Go through a gate beside the farm and follow a track down to the lane with the 'Pen Bryn Bach Restaurant' to the left. Turn left along the lane.

2. Immediately after 'Mynydd Mawr Campsite' on the left and before the car park, bear left on a footpath beside the wall / fence. At the end of the wall bear half-left on a footpath which will take you to the little hilltop of Mynydd y Gwyddel.

This little summit offers extensive views along the coast to the south and inland the hills of Mynydd Anelog, Carn Fadryn and Mynydd Rhiw. But the island of Bardsey, two miles across the sound to the west, will most likely command your attention.

As already mentioned, Bardsey became the goal of pilgrims throughout the Middle Ages and its claim to be the burial place of 20,000 saints gives some idea of the way in which it was viewed during this period. The pilgrimage is thought to have originated during the Dark Ages when monks from the Celtic monastery at Bangor-is-y-coed on the River Dee were massacred by the Saxons of Northumbria under the pagan king Aethelfrith, at the Battle of Chester in AD 616. The monks that escaped fled to the safety of Bardsey deep within Celtic lands and the arduous route that these 'holy men' took through what is now North Wales became enshrined with religious significance, which was to last for almost 1,000 years.

The first religious settlement on the island is thought to have been established by Cadfan who came to Britain with a company of monks in AD 516 having been driven from Brittany by the Franks.

The community that they established was constructed on very simple lines—the monks each had a cell or hut, with a small church enclosed by a wall. This arrangement was called a 'llan' and similar settlements formed the base of many Welsh villages as demonstrated by the prefix 'llan' (Llan—gollen, Llan—bedrog) present in their names today.

It is almost impossible for us to comprehend the simplicity of their life on this remote island today, but the monastic community flourished there for 1,000 years and only came to an end with Henry VIII's Dissolution of the Monasteries in 1536. The lands then passed into the ownership of John Wynn of Bodfel who proved to be very unpopular locally and was said have made a fortune by supporting piracy which was rife at the time.

The island is now owned by Bardsey Island Trust who aim to conserve the island's landscape, historic remains and wildlife. One unusual feature of the island is the lighthouse, which was built in 1821 and has a square tower.

The well and the foundations of St. Mary's Church which lie lower down to the right are traditionally associated with the pilgrimage to Bardsey, being the supposed place where travellers came to pray before making the dangerous crossing. The lack of a safe anchorage in the vicinity and the greater danger of a direct crossing from here make this unlikely, although the size of the foundation does suggest the existence of a large church or monastic building surrounded by enclosed fields—possibly the home of a second monastic settlement during the medieval period.

Facing Bardsey Island, turn half-left down the hillside to a stile in the wall/fence. Follow the path ahead along the edge of the field to a second stile. After this, continue on the obvious path through a more open area.

As you approach a point level with a small rocky islet out to the right turn left and walk up to a stile by a National Trust stone pillar ('Bychestyn') in the upper field boundary. (If you go too far you will reach a deep cliff-lined inlet where you will be forced to turn left. At the fence turn left again to reach the stile.) Go over the stile and follow the field edge ahead to a gate in the far

Looking across to Bardsey from the mainland

corner. Go through the gate and walk ahead to a ladder stile on the right which leads onto the National Trust property at Pen y Cil—Uwchmynydd's southern most headland. Follow the path to the end of the headland.

There is a fine view from here taking in the wide sweep of Aberdaron Bay with its two islands and the headland at Penarfynydd, one of the enclosing arms of the infamous Hell's Mouth. Look westwards for your last glimpse of Bardsey and the treacherous waters of Bardsey Sound.

3. From the cairn head southeast down the slope. About halfway, where the slope levels briefly, look for a path, faint at first, which traverses leftwards along the slope. Take this improving path, soon passing an overgrown walled enclosure on the right.

Beyond Hen Borth, the first little inlet, there are fields on the left and the path becomes more pronounced. Follow this path back to Porth Meudwy and then retrace the outward journey to back to Aberdaron to complete the walk.

7. Tudweiliog
Low cliffs, coves and bays

Easy walking on a gentle section of the coast with wide views

Start: *Park in a layby just south of the village on the B4417 or begin in Tudweiliog. Map reference: SH 237 364.*

Distance: *8.25 kilometres/5½ miles.*

Duration: *Allow 2½-3 hours.*

Difficulty: *Easy. Gentle coastal path, field paths and quiet lanes.*

Food and Drink: *Lion Hotel, Tudweiliog. Food and accommodation, children welcome. 01758 770244.*

Map: *OS 1: 50,000 Landranger 123 Lleyn Peninsula; OS 1:25,000 Explorer 253 Lleyn Peninsula West.*

A LEISURELY AND ATMOSPHERIC STRETCH of unspoilt coast with broad views across the sea towards Ireland, this quiet circuit features the sandy curve of Porth Towyn beach and narrow, flower-filled lanes.

The walk

1. Walk back along the road to Tudweiliog passing the 'Lion Hotel' and about 50 metres beyond the Post Office (almost opposite the church), turn left onto a track between houses, signposted to 'Tyn Llan Caravan Park'. Follow the track to the caravan site and immediately before the site entrance bear right through a kissing gate into fields. Walk ahead along the left-hand edge of two fields to join a farm track. Follow this through Towyn Farm to reach a lane. Take the footpath opposite, which leads past caravans to the beach at Porth Towyn, one of the few sandy beaches on this exposed coast.

2. Turn left immediately after the caravans onto a footpath that follows the top of the coastal slope above the beach, or follow the path down onto the sand and walk left along the beach. Join the coastal path at the far end of the bay.

The coastal path is easily followed now. Continue to a prominent headland where there is a small hut above a cove and fishing boasts pulled up onto the shingle.

This rocky coastline is exposed to westerly gales and has been a hazard to shipping for centuries. The only safe haven on the entire coast is Porth Dinllaen, hidden behind the sheltering arm of Trwyn Porth Dinllaen. In 1864, when the first lifeboat station was established there, some 200 ships had been lost on this coast in just 25 years.

In more recent times, there have been fewer disasters. Today the lifeboat mainly goes to the aid of holiday craft although in 1963 the 314-ton 'St. Trillio' ran aground near Porth Ysgaden in a southwesterly gale. Launched in 1936 by the Liverpool and North Wales Steamship Co., she was en-route from the Bristol Channel to her winter berth at Porth Dinorwic near Bangor when she hit rocks. Three crew members were put ashore by rope ladder, including a 21-year-old stewardess who

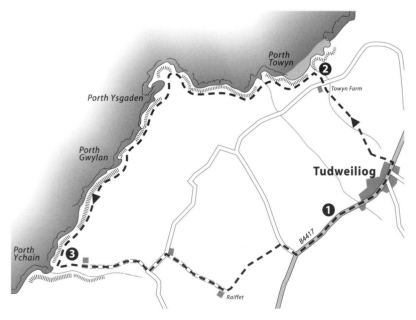

A typical section of Lleyn's north coast

was travelling with the crew of twelve men under Captain Owen Cecil
Williams of Bangor. The remaining crew members were able to refloat
the vessel on the rising tide and although taking in water, she was able
to limp into Porth Dinorwic escorted by the Porth Dinllaen lifeboat.

Continue round into the next cove (Porth Ysgaden), sandy
this time, and join the beach access track. Where this swings left
away from the coast, bear right onto the coastal path again and
follow this over a wide area of open grassy heath bordering the
low cliffs.

The next cove (Porth Gwylan) is rocky and a path on the right
leads down to the shingle beach. Ignore this continuing ahead
on the coastal path for another 1 kilometre / ¾ mile or so to Porth
Ychain where there is a footpath T junction and a cottage visible
over to the left with roof windows (the path right leads down
into the shingle cove).

3. Turn left at the T junction and follow the path towards the
cottage with Carn Fadryn directly behind. The path becomes
enclosed between hedges after a gate. Continue ahead to reach
a lane beside the cottage. Go ahead along the lane contained by
ancient stone walls overgrown with numerous wild flowers.

*These low overgrown walls give the fields a measure of protection
from the almost endless westerly winds which lash this exposed coastline
and allow few trees to grow.*

Turn left at a T junction and after about 300 metres (just before
a house) look for a track on the right carrying a footpath sign.
Follow the track past a large house on the left before turning left
at a kissing gate into fields just before a second house ('Raiffet
Bach'). Keep right around the field edge to a small gate in the
opposite corner. Continue straight ahead now following a line
of kissing gates to a road. Turn right here then left at the B4417
and return to Tudweiliog to complete the walk.

8. Carn Fadryn

Wide views from an isolated hilltop

A heathery climb to panoramic views over the entire peninsula

Start: *Begin the walk at the tiny hamlet of Dinas. This lies just off the Nefyn to Sarn Meyllteyrn road about 8 kilometres/5 miles south of Nefyn. Park by the chapel. Map reference: SH 269 361*

Distance: *10 kilometres/6 miles.*

Duration: *Allow 3 hours.*

Difficulty: *Moderate. The route circles the hill before making the modest climb to the summit. The path to the summit is well walked by locals, but to the north and east the rights of way are less distinct.*

Food and Drink: *No refreshments on the route or nearby.*

Map: *OS 1: 50,000 Landranger 123 Lleyn Peninsula; OS 1:25,000 Explorer 253 Lleyn Peninsula West*

WITH THE EXCEPTION of Yr Eifl, Carn Fadryn is the most striking of Lleyn's hills. Its striking profile is prominent throughout the entire peninsula and as you would expect, the view from the summit is equally extensive.

The walk

1. From the chapel continue to the end of the lane (20 metres) and turn right, signed to 'Llaniestyn, Garnfadryn, Botwnog'. After about 40 metres turn left into a narrow lane contained by high hedges with Carn Fadryn rising directly ahead. The tarmac surface runs out beyond a row of stone cottages and the road becomes a much narrower rough track and eventually a footpath which zig-zags up the hillside for about 700 metres.

The path ends at a gate high up on the hillside below the final heather covered slopes of Carn Fadryn with a small cottage on the right ('Pen y Gorgl'). Turn left here, soon joining a traversing track for about 25 metres before bearing left to a stile to the left of a gateway and just before ruins on the right. Climb the stile and go ahead through a gap in the wall and along a short section of path enclosed between crumbling stone walls to enter a field. The right of way continues through the fields ahead, keeping beside the wall on the right.

Stone steps take you over the walls separating the fields. About 15 metres into the fourth field, turn right over a stone stile in the wall. Turn left along the wall and pass through a young plantation of conifers. At the end of this, a stile leads into a large field ahead.

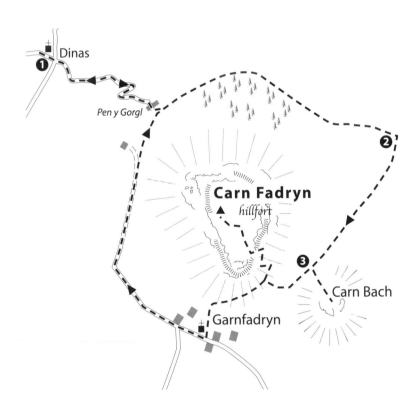

Go ahead through the field. The line of the right of way follows the field boundary on the left but the walked route seems to be directly through the field. After a stile in the fence keep ahead again aiming for a stile almost in the top right corner of the large field ahead.

2. When you reach this don't cross over. Instead, turn right and walk beside the wall. Pass a gateway and in a few metres cross the wall on the left by a ladder stile. Turn right now and rise through a sloping field parallel to the wall.

At the top of the rise you can see both Carn Fadryn and Carn Bach. Aim for the low point on the saddle between these two summits, taking a line which veers away from the wall on your right and leads directly through the field. A gateway should now be visible in a crossing wall just below the skyline, and as you approach this you should be able to see a stile in the corner where the wall and the fence to your left meet.

3. Go over the stile and in a few metres cross the wall on the right by stone steps.

(You can make a short detour to the summit of Carn Bach from here by continuing beside the wall instead of crossing the stile. This is open access land but you must retrace your steps to this point to continue.)

A large field occupies the saddle between the two summits. At the outside corner of a walled field on your left, turn right to a stile in the wall away to the right. Beyond the stile a faint path rises through the bracken to join the main path which zig-zags up to the summit of Carn Fadryn. Turn right and follow the path to the summit.

There are traces on the summit of at least three phases of fortification covering a period of almost 1,500 years. Earliest of these is an Iron Age drystone wall defence thought to date from around 300 BC and enclosing around 5 hectares/12 acres. The existence of a cist burial site within the enclosure indicates that the summit was occupied even earlier. A cairn of stones would have originally covered the cist but

Carn Fadryn

this may well have been removed to provide building materials for the later hillfort defences.

The next building phase is thought to date from around 100 BC and covers almost twice the area of the earlier phase. There are traces of several hut circles at the southern end of the enclosure and outside the wall to the north. When in use it would have been similar in appearance to the remarkable remains of Tre'r Ceiri on Yr Eifl. Like Tre'r Ceiri, occupation is thought to have continued throughout the Iron Age and on into the early Roman period.

The latest defences occupy a small area around the triangulation pillar and are thought to be the remains of a twelfth century Welsh castle. The scant remains give little indication of its appearance but it may have been built in the form of a motte and bailey. The Welsh began to copy the Norman style of castle building around this time and the archeological evidence seems to bear this out. There are no contemporary descriptions of the castle in existence but reference to it was made by Gerald of Wales in 1188. In his book 'The Journey through Wales' he says:

'We crossed the Traeth Mawr and the Traeth Bychan [the estuaries of the Glaslyn and Dwyryd near Porthmadog]. These are two arms of the sea, one large and one small. Two stone castles have been built there recently. The one called Deudraeth belongs to the sons of Cynan and is situated in the Eifionydd area, facing the northern mountains. The second, which is called Carn Madryn, belongs to the sons of Owain: it is on the Lleyn peninsula on the other side of the river, and it faces the sea.'

This is thought to be the fortress of Maredudd ap Cynan one of the grandsons of the better known Owain Gwynedd. Owain and his father, the powerful Gruffydd ap Cynan, were two of the most notable rulers of Gwynedd. It was Gruffydd who restored the ancient dynasty of Maelgwyn Gwynedd.

The isolated position and central location of Carn Fadryn make the view from the summit one of the finest in Lleyn. Much of the northern coast is visible with the sheltering arm of Trwyn Porth Dinllaen near Morfa Nefyn particularly prominent. To the northeast the hills of Carn Boduan and Yr Eifl (The Rivals) can be seen with the mountains of Snowdonia filling the eastern skyline. Much of Cardigan Bay will be visible on a clear day, while the rocky jaws of Hell's Mouth open out to the south.

Retrace your steps down the hillside but follow the path rightwards down to a gate above the village of Garnfadryn. Turn left here and follow the enclosed footpath to a lane.

Turn right along the lane and where it turns left continue straight ahead. After about 400 metres the lane deteriorates into two tarmac strips and eventually grass. A little further on look for the cottage passed earlier ('Pen y Gorgl'). Turn left onto the signed path immediately after the cottage and retrace the outward journey to complete the walk.

9. Porth Dinllaen
Sandy coves, sea views and a pub on the beach

A gentle coastal walk to Lleyn's most unusual settlement, with stunning views across the bay to Yr Eifl/The Rivals

Start: *There is a sizeable National Trust car park at the end of 'Lôn Golff' (Golf Lane) in Morfa Nefyn. Map reference: SH 282 407*

Distance: *7.5 kilometres/4¼ miles.*

Duration: *Allow 2½ hours.*

Difficulty: *Easy. Mainly level coastal walk.*

Food and Drink: *Tŷ Côch, Porth Dinllaen. Not accessible by road; reached either across the golf course or along the beach. Open daily from Easter to October, most Saturdays and some Sunday lunchtimes in winter (But call first in winter). Hot and cold bar food in summer. 01758 720498.*

Map: *OS 1: 50,000 Landranger 123 Lleyn Peninsula; OS 1:25,000 Explorer 253 Lleyn Peninsula West.*

A DELIGHTFUL WALK on gentle footpaths to Lleyn's most unexpected and picturesque settlement. In clear conditions there are stunning views of Yr Eifl (The Rivals) across the bay and inland from the end of the headland.

The walk

1. Turn right out of the car park and follow the road to the golf club and the 'RNLI House'. Go through the kissing gate onto the golf course and follow the narrow tarmac road across the golf course and down to Porth Dinllaen. Rights of way do exist off to the right as you near Porth Dinllaen but they are not waymarked and it is easier to follow the road.

It is hard to believe, as you walk through this tiny remote hamlet, that in the eighteenth and early nineteenth centuries it was set to become one of the busiest sea ports in North Wales and for a time even

Approaching Porth Dinllaen

rivalled Holyhead as the ferry port for Ireland. During this period it had a shipyard and hotels to cater for travellers and plans were laid for rapid expansion.

The sheltered bay, protected from westerly gales by the long promontory of Trwyn Porth Dinllaen, has long been used as an anchorage and as far back as the sixteenth century ships were regularly unloading here. In 1648 the Postmaster General ordered the Irish mail to travel via Porth Dinllaen instead of Holyhead.

By the late eighteenth century plans were afoot to improve the road from Montgomeryshire to Porthmadog, where William Alexander Madocks was shortly to build his great embankment across Traeth Mawr. This had previously acted as a major barrier to communications, involving travellers in a hazardous crossing of the tidal sands or a long detour through difficult mountainous terrain.

With the new road in place and a recently formed Harbour Company, Porth Dinllaen braced itself for great things. Prospects looked even more hopeful when a Parliamentary Bill was introduced to make Porth Dinllaen the packet port for Ireland replacing Holyhead. Holyhead won the day by just one vote!

This was not the end however; with the coming of the railways new hopes were raised and in 1884 a Porth Dinllaen Railway Company was formed and given five years to build the 15 kilometre/9¼ mile track to Pwllheli. For some unknown reason this was never accomplished. The isolated location of Porth Dinllaen and the rapid rise of Holyhead sealed its fate.

Today we can be grateful for its misfortune—this lovely spot has been largely untouched by the twentieth century. The only boats you will see here today are small pleasure craft. And what a location, safe, sheltered waters with an unrivalled backdrop of shapely peaks falling sheer to the sea. The robust, stone-built cottages provide holiday accommodation, and where else can you get a pint on the beach? We can only imagine with horror what the effect would have been on this and the surrounding coastline had Holyhead not won the day.

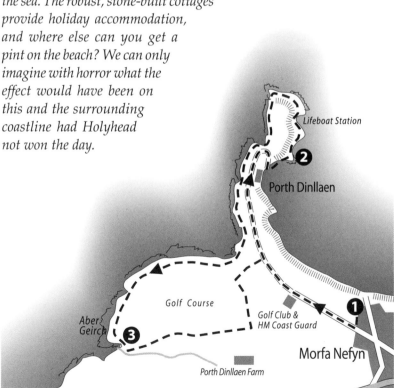

2. Beyond the 'Tŷ Côch Inn' a narrow footpath passes between cottages before continuing just above the high water mark. Pass the lifeboat station and two sandy coves before a slight rise (near a small breakwater) onto a higher path. Continue around the coast which is now more exposed and rugged, before rising to an old lookout tower.

The lookout is well placed with commanding views of Caernarfon Bay—from Holyhead Mountain on Anglesey, to Bardsey on the southwestern tip of Lleyn.

The sheltered bay at Porth Dinllaen is the only safe haven on this entire coast, some 80 kilometres/50 miles of jagged rocks and treacherous sands. In 1864, when the first lifeboat station was established, over 200 ships had been lost in the Port Dinllaen area in just 25 years. By 1881 the lifeboat had made 31 launches and saved 91 lives; even so it received public criticism for failing to go to the aid of the 'SS Cyprian'. This wreck was made famous by the bravery of the captain who sacrificed his own life so that a young stowaway might live.

The 940-ton 'SS Cyprian' was commanded by Captain John Alexander Strachan and had left Liverpool on the 13 October 1881 bound for Genoa. By the time she entered Caernarfon Bay a northwesterly gale was blowing and the ship experienced double engine failure. When both anchors were lost she was doomed and preparations were made to abandon ship. While checking life jackets Captain Strachan noticed a young stranger who had come out of hiding and without hesitating gave the boy his own life jacket.

Shortly afterwards the ship ran aground about 250 metres from the shore near Aber Geirch and began to break up. Captain Strachan was drowned along with eighteen of his crew. They were buried in an unmarked grave at Edern church and Captain Strachan's body was taken to Liverpool.

In memory of Captain Strachan, Mrs Noble of Henley-on-Thames gave £800 to the RNLI to be used for a lifeboat on the Caernarfonshire coast. A new lifeboat station was thus established at Trefor. Appropriately the new craft was named 'Cyprian'.

Looking down onto Porth Dinllaen from the end of the headland

Pass below and to the left of the lookout tower, then keep along the very edge of the golf course. Continue for about 3 kilometres / 1½ miles.

3. At a small bay with a pipeline running into the water, turn inland and cross a stile out of the golf course. Follow the path along a little valley beside the stream ignoring a small footbridge on the right.

Where the path bends to the right go through a kissing gate ahead into fields. Walk beside the fence, with a farm away to the right, and at the next stile drop into a narrow enclosed path. Turn left and follow the path until it opens out onto the golf course. At the end of the bank on your left, turn sharp right and cross the golf course aiming for a large shed beside the road used earlier in the walk. Turn right and retrace the outward journey to complete the walk.

10. Yr Eifl/The Rivals
Up to Tre'r Ceiri, the 'town of the giants'

Stunning around-the-compass panoramas from one of Wales' most impressive and best preserved Iron Age hillforts

Start: *Begin the walk just to the east of the tiny village of Llithfaen. From Llanaelhaearn, on the Caernarfon to Pwllheli road, the B4417 rises steeply to 250 metres above sea level before dropping to Llithfaen. Just beyond this high point, a narrow lane bears to the left and a few cars may be parked on the verge.*
Map reference: SH 367434.

Distance: *5 kilometres/3 miles.*

Duration: *Allow 2½-3 hours.*

Difficulty: *Moderate-difficult. The ascents are moderately strenuous though fairly short as the starting point is already 250 metres. Footpaths are good throughout although a little faint between the summits.*

Food and Drink: *No refreshments on the route. Nearest pub is the Tafarn y Fic community pub, Llithfaen. 01758 750473. Caffi Meinir, Welsh Language and Heritage Centre, Nant Gwrtheyrn. 01758 750442.*

Map: *OS 1: 50,000 Landranger 123 Lleyn Peninsula; OS 1:25,000 Explorer 253 Lleyn Peninsula West*

THERE ARE FEW PLACES IN LLEYN which escape the dramatic profile of Yr Eifl. Seen from the south or west across the pastoral interior they rise as a series of purple cones. From the Caernarfon road they tower above the village of Trefor, and from the graceful bay at Porth Dinllaen they cascade into the sea. Yet the highest top is just 564 metres/1,850 feet and little more than half the height of nearby Snowdon.

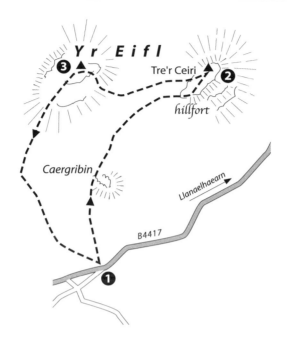

The walk

1. Go through the old iron kissing gate opposite (on the north side of the road) and head directly up the sloping field towards Caergribin, a prominent castellated rock on the skyline. Higher up a ladder stile leads onto the open heather covered moors. As you approach Caergribin the path curves left around the rocks.

Your next objective, Tre'r Ceiri, can be clearly seen now rising to the northeast with its encircling walls. A narrow footpath leads through the heather, soon bearing left to join a more prominent path coming up from Llithfean at a T junction. Turn right here and a little further on cross a stone wall by a large ladder stile. As you approach the final slopes of Tre'r Ceiri keep left at a fork and make the final rise. Enter the enclosure through the obvious entrance at the southwestern end, just above the information board, and make your way through the hut circles on the right-hand edge of the enclosure to the highest point.

Approaching Tre'r Ceiri from Caergribin

Once on the summit you will see that your climb has been well rewarded; not only are you greeted by one of the finest panoramas in Lleyn, but you have before you the most impressive and well preserved Iron Age remains in Wales.

Here you will need little imagination to visualise the settlement as it was, the site is remarkably well preserved and this, along with its vast size may have given rise to the name 'Tre'r Ceiri'—which means 'town of the giants'. The outer walls, some two metres thick and up to five metres high, enclose an area almost 300 metres by 150 metres, and are composed entirely of drystone walling. Within this are the remains of some 150 hut circles of varying size and shape, all well preserved. Of particular note is the survival of the walls almost to their original height. A wall walk and parapet which enabled defenders to patrol the walls is also in amazingly good repair.

The ruins are thought to date from the mid-second century AD, although finds suggest that occupation continued until the end of the fourth century AD. A Bronze Age cairn within the enclosure indicates even earlier use of the site — common with many other hillforts. Some of these sites may have been inhabited continuously throughout the Bronze Age and Iron Age — a period of perhaps 1,000 years or more.

2. From the summit walk north (towards Caernarfon Bay) and bear left to walk beside the wall. Pass a tunnelled exit in the wall and continue to a second paved entrance above the saddle between Tre'r Ceiri and the main summit of Yr Eifl. Leave the enclosure here and bear right to leave through a gap in the lower wall. Turn right immediately and follow a faint footpath which soon curves leftwards through the heather with the main summit directly ahead.

As the hillside becomes steeper, the path turns diagonally-leftwards, eventually joining the main footpath which rises steeply from the left. (Alternatively, reach this point by returning to the stone wall crossed earlier and follow the main path that ascends the hillside to the right).

Turn right and make the short rise to the summit.

As one would expect, the panorama from the highest summit in the group is extensive taking in much of Lleyn's cultivated landscape. The

Hut circles on Tre'r Ceiri

closeness of the sea here exaggerates the height of these little 'mountains', which fall over 500 metres to the waters of Caernarfon Bay.

These steep northern slopes guard the secluded valley of Nant Gwrtheyrn; traditionally held to be the final retreat of Vortigern, the exiled British king who lost control of his kingdom to the Saxons in the fifth century. His troubles resulted from an attempt to enlist the help of Saxon mercenaries to defend his kingdom from the Picts and Irish. His plan worked at first but things turned against him when the Saxons broke the terms of their treaty and began to seize lands and establish their own kingdoms. Vortigern is said to have fled to North Wales and sought refuge in this remote valley from his own people. Today the valley still bears his name—Nant Gwrtheyrn means 'Vortigern's Valley'.

3. From the triangulation pillar a path descends southwest, initially between two small ridges of broken rocks, then through heather with the village of Llithfaen directly ahead. Lower down as the angle begins to ease, cross the faint remains of a drystone wall running at right angles to the path (this is visible from higher up on the hillside). Turn left here and follow a narrow path which runs beside the stone wall with the green dome of Mynydd Garnguwch (the hill with the nipple-like cairn on its summit) rising directly ahead.

Keep ahead where the wall disappears and cross a path that leads down to a cottage by pines on the right. Further on you meet a track, which also leads down to the cottage seen previously. The track forks here. Take the right-hand fork, directly ahead as you approach. This track shortly runs into fields where an old iron ladder stile crosses the fence by a gate. The right of way follows the edge of a depression or gulley running through the centre of the field. Follow this and just before a wall corner, bear left, cross the gulley and head across the field. Aim for a gate in the far fence which soon becomes visible. Continue through the following field to the kissing gate used at the start, to complete the walk.

Northern Snowdonia
Eryri

11. Aberglaslyn & Llyn Dinas
Across the hillsides and along the river

A popular circuit over the hills and back along the riverside via the Aberglaslyn Pass

Start: *Begin the walk at the Nantmor Picnic area where there is ample pay and display parking with toilet facilities.*
Map reference: SH 597 462.

Distance: *9 kilometres/5¾ miles.*

Duration: *Allow 2½-3½ hours.*

Difficulty: *Moderate. Paths are excellent throughout although one section of the Aberglaslyn path requires a short and moderate—but unavoidable—scramble over rocks beside the river.*

Food and Drink: *Three pubs, several restaurants, cafés, and an award-winning ice cream parlour in Beddgelert.*

Map: *OS 1: 50,000 Landranger 115 Snowdon; OS 1:25,000 Explorer/Outdoor Leisure OL 17 Snowdon.*

FINE VIEWS FROM THE HILLSIDES towards the Snowdon Range and Llyn Dinas, contrasted with the riverside return through the picturesque Pass of Aberglaslyn, make this a well-walked and ever-popular circuit.

The walk

1. Walk out of the car park past the toilet block and through the arch under the Welsh Highland Railway. Continue ahead to pick up a path which makes its way up the little valley of Cwm Bychan. At first you pass through woods with the stream to your right before more open ground beyond a gate in the wall.

The path continues up the valley passing numerous remains from mining in the area, from small trial excavations to the rusting supports of an old cableway. Higher up, don't be tempted by

68

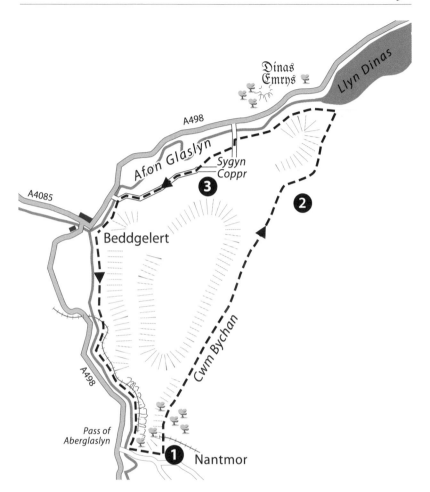

the valley to the left, instead, carry on straight ahead eventually reaching the skyline where a ladder stile leads over the fence.

In clear conditions the view from here is dominated by the southern flanks of Snowdon and its satellite peaks of Yr Aran and Y Lliwedd, while the rocky crest of Crib Goch can be see through the gap known as Bwlch y Saethiau, meaning 'pass of the arrows'. This name links it with the last battle of King Arthur. The pass is one of the supposed sites of his final conflict with Mordred.

Snowdon and Y Lliwedd from the path above Llyn Dinas

2. Turn left here and follow the path to a junction where there is a fingerpost. Turn right signed to 'Llyn Dinas' and follow the well-constructed footpath down hill. Just above the lake the path steepens and zig-zags down to the water's edge.

Llyn Dinas means 'lake of the city' or 'fortress' and is almost certainly a reference to nearby Dinas Emrys, one of the most important Dark Age sites in this part of Wales. It is known to have been the site of a timber castle in the early post-Roman period and there are remains of even earlier, possibly Iron Age, defences. The scant remains to be found on the hilltop today are thought to be those of a thirteenth century stone tower.

Turn left by the outflow of the lake through a kissing gate and, ignoring the footbridge on the right, follow a good path ahead beside the river with the flat-topped hill of Dinas Emrys ahead.

Although little is known about the occupants of Dinas Emrys for sure, it would almost certainly have been used by the many Welsh Princes prior to the Edwardian Conquest, although the need for a stronghold this far into the mountains can not have been great once the threat from Irish raids had been removed.

Dinas Emrys is the location of the mythical confrontation between Vortigern, the high king of Britain and Ambrosius (Emrys in Welsh) the British leader responsible for Vortigern's exile and leader of the British resistance to the Saxon colonisation of eastern Britain.

Pass a stone-built house on the left and eventually join the access road to 'Sygyn Coppr' (copper mine). Bear left with the road, and keep ahead ignoring the left fork to the car park. Immediately after the road passes through a gap in the wall, turn right onto a footpath which runs beside the wall. The path eventually joins a narrow tarmac lane.

3. Turn right and walk along the lane, passing a campsite on the right, until it bends right over the river to join the A498.

Here, immediately before the bridge, stone steps lead left over the wall and onto a riverside footpath. Stay on this path, crossing an access road, and continuing ahead until you come to the metal footbridge in Beddgelert where Afon Glaslyn and Afon Colwyn meet. Do not cross the river (unless visiting Beddgelert), instead, turn left and keep beside the river on the good footpath.

At the Welsh Highland Railway (almost 1 kilometre / ¾ mile), cross by the level crossing and follow the footpath which has recently been improved beside the river. As the path enters the gorge of Aberglaslyn the railway disappears into a tunnel and the path follows constructed walkways, which take you over rocky sections above the river. This is a lovely part of the walk.

The Pass of Aberglaslyn is a well known beauty spot, made popular by Victorian travellers, writers and painters. It is almost impossible to find a book about North Wales, particularly from the early half of the twentieth century, which does not contain a photograph from the bridge at the mouth of the gorge.

As you emerge from the gorge at Aberglaslyn, do not go through the kissing gate onto the road. Instead, turn left and follow the woodland path back to the car park at Nantmor to complete the walk.

Aberglaslyn Pass

12. Llyn Gwynant
Mirror in the mountains

Aound a beautiful mountain lake with stunning views of Snowdon

Start: *Begin the walk at the National Park car park for the Watkin Path approach to Snowdon. This lies between Llyn Dinas and Llyn Gwynant on the A498. Map reference: SH 628 507.*

Distance: *9 kilometres/5½ miles.*

Duration: *Allow 3-4 hours.*

Difficulty: *Moderate. Good footpaths throughout.*

Food and Drink: *Nearby pubs and cafés in Beddgelert. Or, try the famous climbers'Pen-y-Gwryd Hotel at the junction of the A498 and A 4086. 01286 870211. Lovely picnic spots above the lake.*

Map: *OS 1: 50,000 Landranger 115 Snowdon; OS 1:25,000 Explorer/Outdoor Leisure OL 17 Snowdon.*

A BEAUTIFUL MOUNTAIN LAKE surrounded by Snowdonia's highest tops creates the perfect setting for stunning views later in the walk dominated by Wales' highest peak—Snowdon.

The walk

1. Turn left out of the car park, cross the bridge and in about 100 metres or so turn right into a narrow lane. Snowdon's Watkin Path starts here, entering the woods on the signed footpath ahead. Ignore this, walking along the lane instead to the footbridge on the right, in about 100 metres. Cross the footbridge and follow an attractive riverside footpath with views left across the meadows of Nantgwynant to Snowdon.

At the end of the path where the river bends, cross a second footbridge. Turn left for about 35 metres, then bear right through a gap in the wall. Walk ahead, slightly left of centre, through the following field to the top corner of the field where there are two gaps in the wall. Go through the left-hand gap where a grass track passes through the wall. The track curves left here, but the path goes ahead parallel to the wall on the right, to the top corner of the field, where there is an old iron gate on the right. Go through the gate and follow an old pathway enclosed by stone walls.

Within 150 metres, the path turns right, enclosed by ruined walls now. Follow the path down to an old stone barn on the left ('Ysgubor Bwlch').

Cross the ladder stile by the gate and walk beside the river on a well-used footpath. Where the path swings right towards an old house, go ahead, passing to the left of a small tree-covered knoll, to a gap in the wall. The path now rises to a mound of rust covered stones—the waste from a small trial mine nearby. It is also an excellent spot to look for samples of iron pyrites or 'Fool's Gold'.

The well-worn footpath continues to rise before descending a delightful secluded valley to pass a small ruin over to

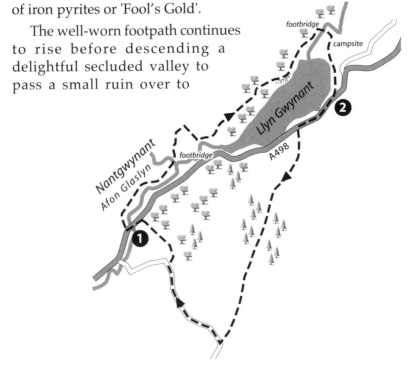

View to the southern flanks of Snowdon near the end of the walk

the right. Cross a stile and a stream a little further on, then rise through the trees to a spectacular viewpoint overlooking the lake. The path descends from here to a ladder stile over the wall close to the point at which Afon Glaslyn enters the lake. Cross the stile and continue with the wall to your right, eventually passing through an area of huge fallen rocks. Turn right just beyond this over the footbridge, which takes you into a campsite occupying the flat green fields at the head of the lake. Walk straight ahead to a ladder stile (but don't cross it), then turn right, following a fence line down to the water's edge. Turn left along the shore and follow the footpath to the road (A498).

This dramatic valley has been used as the setting for a number of film productions, notably First Knight *with Richard Gere and Sean Connery, and* Merlin, *a TV production. Ironically, there is little of historic interest here today — no major events are known to have taken place here and the only early remains consist of a Roman camp at the head of the valley near Pen y Gwryd and the Dark Age fortress which existed at Dinas Emrys further down the valley towards Beddgelert.*

One reason may be its location, deep within the mountain wilderness of Eryri in the heart of the ancient kingdom of Gwynedd. As such it would undoubtedly have been used as a safe retreat by the people of Gwynedd in times of trouble.

2. Turn right along the road and, after about 500 metres, look for a signed footpath on the left immediately after a milestone built into the wall. This follows a stony track beyond a gate which begins to rise before veering right after 150 metres or so. Leave the track here and go ahead up stone steps to walk beside the wall on the left. Higher up, where you meet the track again on a bend, keep ahead beside the wall as before.

Continue beside the wall to meet the track again—which you should now follow. The angle eases as you climb. Continue, to pass through a gateway in the wall, and follow the track as it bends right towards farm buildings. Ignore the signed footpath to the right immediately before the buildings which will take you down to the Youth Hostel. Instead, turn left along the track through a gateway in the wall. Follow the track/path towards woods where, in about 75 metres, it swings left into the trees. The path is well-worn and heads directly through the woods for almost 1 kilometre/¾ mile.

A ladder stile takes you out of the trees and into an area of rhododendrons. The footpath ahead is still obvious and eventually leads to a gate in the wall on the left. Go through the gate, over a small sleeper footbridge and continue ahead through grazing fields. Cross Afon Llynedno by a wooden footbridge and bear left along a track to emerge in a quiet lane. Turn right and walk down the lane with dramatic views of the Snowdon group directly ahead.

After about 1.5 kilometres/1 mile, bear right onto a signed footpath into woods again. An overgrown stone bridge takes you over the river and up to a T junction with an access road. Turn left here and follow the road back to the car park to complete the walk.

13. Capel Curig

A mirror in the heart of the mountains

A beautiful walk visiting one of the most famous lakeside viewpoints in Britain

Start: *Begin the walk from the car park situated behind the shops in Capel Curig. Map ref SH 720 582.*

Distance: *7 kilometres/4¼ miles.*

Duration: *Allow 2-2½ hours.*

Difficulty: *Easy. Excellent paths throughout.*

Food and Drink: *Nearby pubs and cafés in Capel Curig. Lovely picnic spots by the lake.*

Map: *OS 1: 50,000 Landranger 115 Snowdon; OS 1:25,000 Explorer/Outdoor Leisure OL 17 Snowdon.*

HERE ARE TWO CLASSIC VIEWS TO DIE FOR in one short, easy walk: the complete Snowdon Horseshoe reflected in the tranquil waters of Llyn Mymbyr, and a wider, more elevated panorama from the Capel Curig Pinnacles.

The walk

1. Turn left out of the car park and walk over the old bridge to join the road with shops to your left. Turn half-left, cross the A5 and take the signed footpath directly opposite beside the war memorial. This rises through grazing fields towards the small rocky peak which overlooks Capel Curig (Capel Curig Pinnacles) and gives a classic view of the Snowdon group rising beyond Llynnau Mymbyr. The path passes to the left of the rocks, eventually entering woods by a stile or gate. Follow the clear footpath ahead through the trees, then across the bracken covered hillside below Clogwyn Mawr. Climb over a ladder stile and continue ahead on the path to pass through a gap in a ruined stone wall. Bear right off the main path in a few paces to cross a stone footbridge over the stream and make your way rightwards crossing a second smaller footbridge.

Pass the gate on your left and keep beside the garden to cross a ladder stile lower down. Turn left by the fence and follow a faint grass track which leads in a few metres to a gate onto a rough access road beside 'Bryn Tyrch Uchaf'. Go through the gate and bear left along the track for a few metres, then bear left again to follow a path beside the fence on your left. Pass above an old wooden chalet to reach a ladder stile. Cross the stile and continue straight ahead through a gap in a wall of large boulders, crossing a farm track and continuing ahead down to a ladder stile leading into woods. Follow the clear footpath down through the trees.

Ignore a path to the right lower down, continuing ahead on a contouring path. Pass a small stone building on the left and, a little further on, meet a rising track at a T junction. Turn left up the hill and after passing through a gap in a stone wall look for an obvious path on the right. Follow this path with good views both into and along the valley and across to Moel Siabod. Continue to a T junction with a footpath near a small cottage on

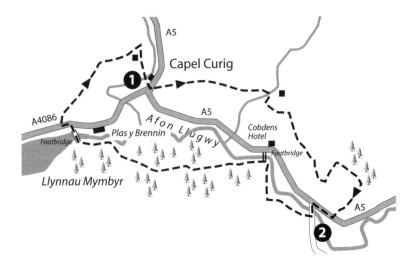

The classic view of Snowdon from Llynnau Mymbyr

the left. Turn right down the hill to a stile which leads to a car park by Bryn Glo café.

2. Turn right along the main road (A5). Shortly, turn left over the old stone bridge and take the signed footpath on the right almost immediately, which follows an access road for a few metres before bearing right down the bank. Cross the footbridge and go ahead across a field to the river. Bear left now and walk beside the river.

In the corner of the last field, a ladder stile takes you into woods. Follow the riverside footpath ahead, then, in a few metres turn left away from the river (the riverside footpath continues ahead to a footbridge) and follow a footpath up a tiny 'valley' or depression with high rocks on its right-hand side. At the top of the rise, join a path which rises from the right, turn left through 'slits' in the rock and follow the path with the river and the A5 down to your right.

Continue on the good forest path to a T junction with a forest road. Turn left here, then bear right shortly at a fork and follow the forest road to 'Bryn Engan', a large house on the right. Go through the gate straight ahead and continue to the footbridge at Plas-y-Brenin (meaning 'King's Palace' or 'Hall) Outdoor Education Centre.

Plas-y-Brenin is now a well established outdoor pursuits centre but was originally built as a sixty-room hotel during the first decade of the nineteenth century when it was known as 'The Royal Hotel'. It was built by Lord Penrhyn who owned the Penrhyn slate quarries at Bethesda and who was responsible for building the first coach road through the Ogwen Valley between 1791 and 1800, where previously there had only been a packhorse trail. By 1803 the Capel Curig Turnpike Trust had built a link road from Capel Curig through Betws-y-Coed to Pentrefoelas, and London to Holyhead coaches immediately began to use this instead of the longer and more hazardous alternative through Conwy and along the coast. The hotel would thus have originally catered for those travelling between London and Ireland.

In 1815 Thomas Telford was commissioned to improve the entire London to Holyhead road as several sections had gradients of 1 in 6, which meant difficult and dangerous travelling for coaches (second class travellers were obliged to get out and push on the steeper sections). For the most part, he followed the same line as the existing route through the mountains, passing through both Betws-y-Coed and Capel Curig. The Irish mail coaches used this route regularly until the building of the railways. By then, however, both Capel Curig and Betws-y-Coed had been placed firmly on the tourist map and have continued to cater for visitors ever since.

Cross the footbridge and rise to the road. Turn left and after 150 metres or so, turn right over a ladder stile. The path bears half-left from the stile for about 20 metres, before curving right to contour the hillside (ignore a farm track on the right). Continue to join a rough farm road after a cottage on the right. Turn right here and return to Capel Curig to complete the walk.

14. Llugwy valley
Above the tumbling Afon Llugwy

Wooded hillsides and wide views either side of Afon Llugwy between Capel Curig and Betws-y-Coed

Start: *Begin the walk at Pont-y-Pair, the old stone bridge which carries the B5106 over Afon Llugwy in the centre of Betws-y-Coed. Map reference: SH 791 567. Parking is available at a number of car parks throughout the village. For a shorter circuit, begin at the forest car park on the A5 at 'Cae'n y Coed', midway between the Swallow Falls and The Ugly House/Tŷ Hyll. Map reference: SH 763 576.*

Distance: *10.5 kilometres/6½ miles.*

Duration: *Allow 3-3½ hours.*

Difficulty: *Moderate. Some steep ascents. Riverside paths and forest tracks are excellent throughout.*

Food and Drink: *Numerous pubs, restaurants, cafés and a fish and chip shop in Betws-y-Coed. Royal Oak Hotel/Stables Bar with large covered outdoor area. Real ales and extensive menu with specials board. Walkers and children welcome. 01690 710219.*

Map: *OS 1: 50,000 Landranger 115 Snowdon; OS 1:25,000 Explorer/Outdoor Leisure OL 17 Snowdon.*

SILENT FORESTS AND RUSHING WATERS define this varied circuit of the Llugwy valley above Betwys-y-Coed. Highlights include the Miners' Bridge, Swallow Falls, Ugly House, and ancient Sarn Helen—probably Wales' best-known Roman road.

The walk

1. From the A5 in the centre of Betws-y-Coed cross the bridge and turn left immediately. After about 50 metres there is a pay and display car park on your right; bear left immediately after this onto the riverside footpath ('Mynydd y Coed All Ability Trail').

The first section of the path is a raised wooden walkway followed by a surfaced path. This leads to picnic tables close to the river (in about 350 metres) after which the paths swings right. Go ahead at this point, off the surfaced path and past the picnic tables to locate a ladder stile hidden behind rocks immediately adjacent to the river. Go to the left of the rocks to reach the stile. Cross the stile and follow the path through the following fields close to the river on the left.

After the fields, enter woods again and continue ahead on the riverside path to a large wooden footbridge spanning the river known as the 'Miner's Bridge'.

The name of this bridge recalls the occupation of many of the locals when lead mining was carried out in the hills to the north during the nineteenth century. The original bridge provided a short-cut for miners living at Pentre Du on the south side of the river, saving them the mile and a half walk via the old bridge at Betws-y-Coed.

Do not cross the Miner's Bridge; instead, bear right on the footpath which heads directly up the hillside to a lane. Follow the signed footpath opposite. This well used and obvious footpath runs diagonally up the hillside with glimpses of the deepening valley to your left through the trees.

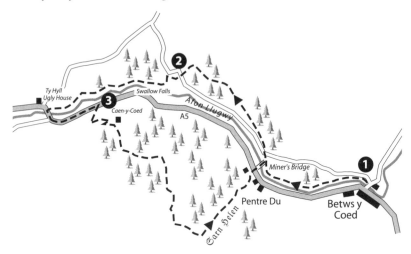

The view west along the Llugwy Valley to Moel Siabod and Snowdon

At the top of the rise cross a stile into a small field. Follow the path ahead with a wall on the left to the corner of a cottage garden, also on the left. Bear right on a grass path here, passing small wall-enclosed fields on the left to a rough access road. Turn left along the road and, immediately after a ruined stone barn, turn right through the centre of a field. A gate and stile lead into woods. There are two paths here—take the path ahead (ignore the one on the right) and follow this down through the trees. Lower down the path runs beside a stone wall with fields on the left and a fine view of the wooded Llugwy Valley and Moel Siabod ahead.

Keep beside the wall, passing a gate. Where the wall makes a ninety degree turn to the left, follow the path as it swings left down through the trees to a stile in the lower corner. Cross the stile and walk down to a second stile which leads onto a short path beside a cottage garden to enter a lane.

2. Turn right up the lane for about 100 metres or so and, just before the bridge over a stream, turn sharp left onto a descending path. Follow this down below the lane to a T junction. Turn right here onto a good forest footpath, which soon crosses a footbridge over the stream. Follow the signed path, which bears left after the bridge, and descends to meet a forest track. Go right along this track for about 30 metres, before bearing left on a path that soon crosses a wooden footbridge over a stream.

A little further on you will be aware of the river which can be both seen and heard amid the trees down to the left. Ignore a prominent forest track on the right here; instead, keep ahead on the path that crosses the steep rocky wall of the gorge high above Afon Llugwy. There are good views of the Swallow Falls from a small viewing area here, or you can continue ahead to a point where you can look down on the famous cascade.

The Swallow Falls are probably the most famous falls in North Wales although they are neither the highest nor the most spectacular. Their popularity has its origins in the establishment of Betws-y-Coed as a tourist destination during the nineteenth century. The original name of the falls was Rhaeadr Ewynnol, which means 'foaming falls', but the name seems to have been mistaken by the Victorians for the similar word, Rhaeadr-y-Wennol, which means 'swallow falls'.

Beyond the falls a good footpath stays close to the river, to eventually enter grazing fields. Continue ahead beside the river and just before the far end of the field, turn left over a stile in the wall. Walk along the wooded river bank now to the old stone bridge carrying the A5. Steps lead up onto the bridge beside the famous stone cottage known as the 'Ugly House' ('Tŷ Hyll').

The Ugly House is said to be the result of a local law which stated that if a house could be built between sunset and sunrise the builders could claim the house and the land it was built on.

Turn left over the bridge and walk along the road for just under 1 kilometre / ¾ mile to the forest car park (Cae'n y Coed) on the right.

3. Turn right here and take the forest road which rises sharply to the right. Where this swings back to the left, bear right onto a long straight forest road, which rises steadily through the trees. Almost at the top of the rise, and immediately before a stream, bear left onto a footpath that continues the climb to a gate and cattle grid leading into fields. Go through the gate and follow the faint grass track ahead to a small farm. Enter the farmyard by a stile to the right of outbuildings. Leave the yard by a large gate ahead to the right of the house. Go through this and follow the rising grass track behind the farmhouse.

At the top of the rise, pass through a gate near a stone barn and continue on the faint track to a stile and gate which lead onto a forest road. Turn left here and follow this road as it contours round the hillside. Keep left at the first junction and bear right at a T junction a little further on.

Follow a good forest road now to a fork beneath power cables (almost 1 kilometre / ¾ mile). Bear right here and after about 300 metres, opposite a lane on the right, turn left onto a descending path / track between stone walls.

This path is part of Sarn Helen the Roman road which linked the forts of Caerhun in the Conwy Valley and Tomen-y-Muir near Trawsfynydd. The Romans often formalised existing routes and tracks, particularly in difficult terrain. This route over the hills may well have been in use for many centuries before the Romans came here.

At a forest road with a cottage on the right, continue the descent straight ahead to emerge in the settlement of Pentre Du. Cross the A5 and take the path opposite down to the Miner's Bridge. Cross the bridge, turn right and follow the riverside path back to Betws-y-Coed to complete the walk.

15. Llyn Idwal & Llyn Ogwen
Spectacular glaciated mountain scenery

A rugged walk to two beautiful mountain lakes

Start: *Parking is available in a large layby at the eastern end of Llyn Ogwen on the A5. Map reference: SH 666 605.*

Distance: *9 kilometres/5½ miles.*

Duration: *Allow 3-4 hours.*

Difficulty: *Hard. Stamina required. Although footpaths are reasonable throughout, this is the toughest walk in the book and shouldn't be attempted in lightweight footwear. The route is best avoided in poor weather.*

Food and Drink: *Small café in the National Trust and Countryside Council for Wales managed car park on the A5 at the west end of Llyn Ogwen.*

Map: *OS 1: 50,000 Landranger 115 Snowdon; OS 1:25,000 Explorer/Outdoor Leisure OL 17 Snowdon.*

SHAPED BY ANCIENT GLACIERS, Llyn Ogwen, Llyn Idwal and the Devil's Kitchen at the head of Cwm Idwal form the backdrop for this demanding but rewarding circuit through some of Snowdonia's most dramatic scenery.

The walk

1. From the layby, cross the river by the stone bridge and pass through a small group of pines. Pass 'Glan Denna' on the left and continue over the cattle grid on the farm track towards 'Tal-y-Llyn Ogwen' farm.

Just before the farm, turn right on the signed path beside the wall. At a stile on the left cross the wall. The well-made path to Cwm Ffynnon Lloer bends right up beside the stream here. Don't take this path, keep straight ahead on a less distinct

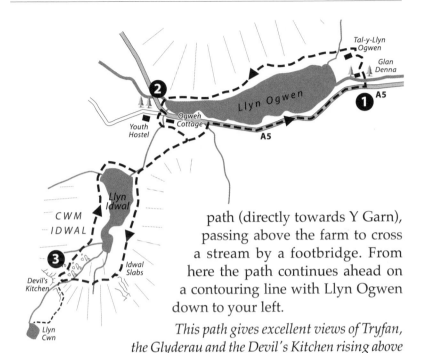

path (directly towards Y Garn), passing above the farm to cross a stream by a footbridge. From here the path continues ahead on a contouring line with Llyn Ogwen down to your left.

This path gives excellent views of Tryfan, the Glyderau and the Devil's Kitchen rising above Cwm Idwal at the end of the lake. These shady north facing cwms are the result of small hanging glaciers, which lingered on the northern slopes of the mountains at the end of the last Ice Age. The result is the dramatic contrast between the craggy northeastern and the more gentle southwestern slopes of all the mountains in Britain.

Part way along the path there is an area of easy angled slabs that tumble down towards the lake shore. These slabs have been polished smooth by the belly of a massive glacier, which would have filled the entire valley to a depth of perhaps 500 metres or more during the last Ice Age. This glacier is thought to have been one of numerous 'tongues' of ice forced through the mountains by the weight of an enormous ice cap situated to the east. These 'tongues' or 'fingers' of ice are also responsible for the present form of valleys such as nearby Nant Ffrancon, the Llanberis Pass, Nant Gwynant and the Conwy Valley.

Beyond the slabs, the path continues, gradually dropping, to eventually run close to the shore of the lake.

Llyn Idwal and the Devil's Kitchen

2. Near the end of the lake, make your way through an area of huge boulders to reach the road (A5). Turn left and walk along the road to Ogwen Cottage (Outdoor Pursuits Centre, Mountain Rescue Post and Youth Hostel). Turn right into the car park (toilets and snack bar) then bear left onto the Llyn Idwal path immediately before the toilets.

The path is well used and, after crossing the stream, heads towards the bwlch between Tryfan and Glyder Fach before reaching a fork. Keep right with the main path, soon reaching the northern shore of Llyn Idwal.

You will have been aware of the dark brooding cliffs at the head of the lake and the huge cleft known as the 'Devil's Kitchen' for some time on the approach, but as you reach the lake the whole dramatic scene opens out. Despite being one of the wildest and most impressive cwms in Snowdonia, Cwm Idwal is probably one of the most accessible.

It was here in Cwm Idwal that the glacial origin of much of our highland landscape was first recognised. This discovery was made by Charles Darwin, best known for his theories on evolution; but Darwin was in fact a geologist rather than a biologist and made several visits to Cwm Idwal to study the unique landscape and its rock structure.

The rocks of the cwm are mainly volcanic, thought to be 450 million years old and are distorted into a huge 'U' shaped fold—known as the 'Idwal Syncline'—which can be seen in rock layers forming the distinctive terraces that curve upwards on either side of the Devil's Kitchen. The present form of the cwm, however, owes its existence to much more recent events—the action of ice during the last Ice Age. Evidence suggests that at its greatest extent ice spilled over from above the Devil's Kitchen and flowed down into the cwm in the form of an ice tongue up to 500 metres thick, which then joined the main Ogwen/Nant Ffrancon glacier, possibly deflecting the latter and causing it to turn through almost 90 degrees. The result—Nant Ffrancon—is one of the most spectacular legacies from the Ice Age in Wales. As the ice dwindled, it left behind the mounds of debris known as 'moraines', which can be seen on the far side of the lake and are passed later in the walk.

Follow the path ahead along the eastern shore, passing the foot of the Idwal Slabs, which form the northern face of Glyder Fawr. From here the path steepens to pass through the chaos of enormous boulders torn from the cliffs above. Follow this path to a junction (not all that obvious) near a group of particularly large boulders and with the Devil's Kitchen almost directly above.

3. From here a path continues to climb to the foot of the Devil's Kitchen, then bears left along one of the wide rock terraces, to reach to top of the crags. There is no difficulty on this path other than that already encountered climbing over bouders, but it is strenuous. At the top there are grand views back into Cwm Idwal

Llyn Ogwen

and over to Snowdon. There is also a small lake—Llyn Cŵn—an excellent picnic spot in good weather.

From here, return to the path junction in the boulder field and bear left. (Alternatively, you can miss out the climb to the top by turning right at the junction by the group of large boulders.) Follow the descending path down to the western shore of Llyn Idwal, passing between the moraine ridges mentioned earlier. Continue to the end of the lake.

Turn right along the shingle shore and cross the footbridge over the outflow to reach the path used earlier. Turn left and head back towards Ogwen Cottage. Where the path swings left, bear right—not onto the most obvious path that climbs up towards Tryfan and Glyder Fach, but a little to the left of this where a faint path takes a diagonal line over open ground down towards the road. A number of stiles cross the wall to reach the road. Turn right along the road to complete the walk.

16. Dolwyddelan

A Roman road and a native Welsh castle

Along ancient 'Sarn Helen' into a hidden valley and over the hills to medieval Castell Dolwyddelan

Start: *Begin the walk in Dolwyddelan. There is free parking in the signed car park near Dolwyddelan railway station. Take the road opposite the Post Office in the centre of Dolwyddelan; the car park is on the left immediately after the bridge over Afon Lledr.*
Map reference: SH 737 521.

Distance: *9.5 kilometres/6 miles.*

Duration: *Allow 3-4 hours.*

Difficulty: *Moderate. Paths are generally good, with one steep section in the climb out of Cwm Penamnen.*

Food and Drink: *Y Gwdyr Hotel, High Street, Dolwyddelan. Real ales and home-cooked food. Beer garden. Free wi-fi access. 01690 750209. Also coffee from the Spar shop in the village centre.*

Map: *OS 1: 50,000 Landranger 115 Snowdon; OS 1:25,000 Explorer/Outdoor Leisure OL 18 Harlech, Portmadog & Bala.*

STEP BACK INTO ROMAN AND MEDIEVAL WALES in this intriguing circuit around the Lledr Valley and little-known Cwm Penamnen, traversing sections of the Sarn Helen Roman road and visiting native Welsh Castell Dolwyddelan.

The walk

1. Walk back to the road and turn left over the railway. Turn right immediately after the bridge and follow the road as it rises out of the village and into the hidden valley of Cwm Penamnen with the cascading river down to the left.

As you enter the cwm the lane levels and you pass the excavated ruins of Tai Penamnen, a house dating back to the early fifteenth century.

Tai Penamnen was the seat of Maredudd ap Ieuan, founder of the Gwyns of Gwydir (see pages 94 & 95).

This lane follows the line of the old Roman road which linked the forts of Caerhun in the Conwy Valley and Tomen-y-Muir near Trawsfynydd. Throughout the Dark Ages it continued to provide the main communication route with the south. The armies of the two Llywelyns, along with their famous ancestors, Owain Gwynedd and Gruffydd ap Cynan, would all have marched this way to conflicts in South Wales and the southern borders.

Continue along the lane for about 1 kilometre / ¾ mile passing the track to 'Gwyndy', a farmhouse on the left. A little further on and immediately before a cottage on the left ('Tan y Bwlch'),

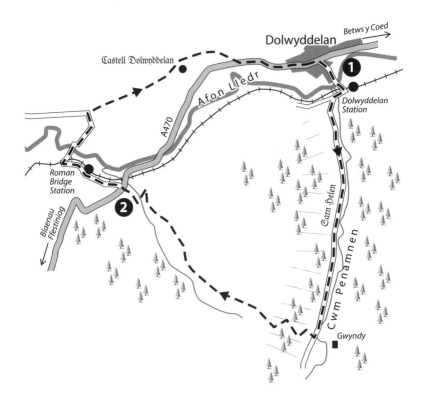

take the signed footpath on the right. This climbs steeply and directly up the hillside to a forest road. Across the road, the path continues to rise steeply through the trees. A stile at the end of the climb takes you onto the open hillside and you are treated to a grand view across the valley to the Moel Siabod, with the backs of the Glyderau and the Snowdon group to the left.

Follow the footpath ahead directly down the hillside. Lower down the path merges into a more defined farm track. Remain on this track, passing ruins (possibly 'hafods' or summer dwellings from earlier centuries) and going through gates.

Stay with the track until you can see a number of stone houses over to the left beyond a small valley and stream. A little further on, after the next gate enter a smaller field with house roofs visible ahead (roughly 200 metres away) and the castle on the far hillside. About 75 metres after the gate, take the signed footpath on the left (marked by small posts) to a ladder stile by a gate. Pass through a small field, then cross an old stone footbridge over the river. The path now keeps close to the river on the right to eventually meet the road. Turn right to the A470.

The present A470 over the Crimea Pass was only built in the mid-nineteenth century and was named by the soldiers who built it who had recently returned from the Crimean War. The desolate moors between the Lledr Valley and Blaenau Ffestiniog evidently reminded them of the land in which they had fought.

2. Cross the road and follow the lane opposite, signed 'Roman Bridge'. This leads past Roman Bridge railway station, then over the railway and the river. Continue along the rising lane ignoring signed footpaths, first on the left, then on the right, until you reach a farm where the lane bends sharp left. Turn right here onto a signed footpath. At first you follow a track with gates and stiles then, where this bends left (about 500 metres), bear right as indicated by a finger post, onto a grassy path. Pass through a gate in a few metres then continue straight ahead on the obvious footpath.

Castell Dolwyddelan

Soon the castle comes into view and the path drops into a dip to join a concrete road to the left of, and a little beyond the castle.

Castell Dolwyddelan is one of the few native Welsh castles from the period of the independent Princes still in existence. Most castles built prior to the Edwardian Conquest were made from timber and have long since disappeared. In the case of Dolwyddelan, the original wooden structure, built about 1170 by Iorwerth Drwyndwn, Lord of Nant Conwy and father of Llywelyn the Great, was replaced by stone—an increasingly common practice among the Normans at that time. Llywelyn is thought to have been born here in 1173 but was removed as an infant for safe upbringing in Powys, the land of his mother, when his father was killed. When he returned to take control of the Kingdom of Gwynedd in 1195, Dolwyddelan became one of his main strongholds.

The castle was used extensively throughout the thirteenth century by both Llywelyn the Great and his grandson, sometimes referred to as 'Llywelyn the Last' (being the last independent Welsh prince) in their wars with both the English kings and Welsh rivals. Dolwyddelan finally fell to the armies of Edward I in 1283 after a two-month winter siege following the death of Llywelyn at Builth Wells. Although there were a few minor battles still to be fought, the fall of Dolwyddelan is generally accepted as signalling the end of Welsh resistance to Edward I.

The present structure dates from the fifteenth century when an extra floor was added giving the tower is square top and battlements. In 1489 the castle was acquired by Maredudd ap Ieuan, an ancestor of the Wynns of Gwydir. The name Wynn was derived from 'Ieuan' in Tudor times when the English fashion for surnames was being followed by the Welsh gentry. Maredudd is said to have been responsible for the building of St Gwyddelon's church in Dolwyddelan to replace an earlier church with the same dedication. The new church was said to have been more visible from Maredudd's new house (Tai Penamnen) in Cwm Penamnen, and more easily defended. The reason for this precaution seems to have been the nearby hospice of Ysbyty Ifan. This was an area of sanctuary run by the Knights of the Order of St John of Jerusalem over which the king's officials had no authority or right of entry. Over the centuries it had attracted all manner of outlaws and undesirables who began to prey on the surrounding areas. Maredudd thus felt vulnerable in his mountain valley and he is said to have attended church accompanied by a small army.

It may have been for this reason that Maredudd bought and moved to Gwydir near Llanrwst in the Conwy Valley in 1500. His son, John Wynn, was the first to use the name which was to become synonymous, not just with Gwydir, but most of the Conwy Valley. In the nineteenth century the ruins of Dolwyddelan were renovated by Lord Willoughby de Eresby, a descendant of Maredudd ap Ieuan.

Follow the concrete road past the castle and where this turns sharp right go through the gate/gateway ahead and continue along an unmade lane to the road A470. Turn left and return to Dolwyddelan where a right turn at the Post Office will take you back to the car park to complete the walk.

17. Aber Falls

Up to the Waterfall

Through riverside woods to one of North Wales' highest and
most impressive waterfalls

Start: *Take the minor road which runs south from the A55 through
Abergwyngregyn to the Aber Falls and park immediately before the
bridge, at 'Coedydd Aber Nature Reserve'.*
Map reference: SH 663 720.

Distance: *9.5 kilometres/6 miles.*

Duration: *Allow 3-4 hours.*

Difficulty: *Moderate. Footpaths are good throughout.*

Food and Drink: *No refreshments nearby.*

Map: *OS 1: 50,000 Landranger 115 Snowdon; OS 1:25,000
Explorer/Outdoor Leisure OL 17 Snowdon.*

HIDDEN IN THE MOUNTAINOUS FOLDS of the northern Carneddau
is the spectacular Aber Falls/Rhaeadr Fawr—one of Wales'
highest waterfalls.

The walk

1. Take the signed path to the Aber Falls, which leaves the lane
immediately before the bridge. The path follows the right bank
of the river at first, before crossing a footbridge. Go through a
kissing gate and turn right onto a broad obvious track. This track
runs parallel to the river and takes you straight to the Aber Falls.
(about 3.5 kilometres / 1¾ miles).

(An alternative path is signed to the left just before a small
cottage—'Nant Rhaeadr', which houses an exhibition open to the
public between April and September. The path makes its way
along the edge of the plantations on the left and could be used
in conjunction with the main path for a shorter walk.)

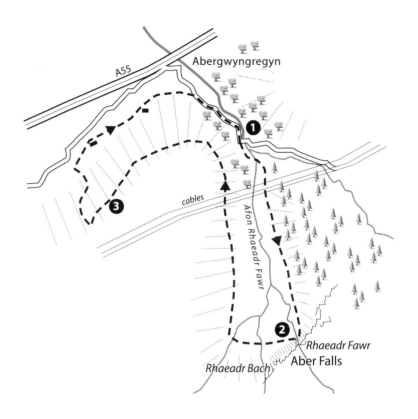

The falls can be seen for some time on the approach—one of Wales' highest waterfalls. Afon Goch drains large areas of the northern Carneddau and can be very impressive while in full flood.

2. Cross the footbridge below the falls and bear right to a ladder stile over the wall, signed for the 'North Wales Path' (NWP). The next section of the route follows the North Wales Path. Follow the obvious and well-used path along the foot of the hillside crossing a second footbridge below Rhaeadr Bach—the aptly named 'little waterfall'. Beyond this, turn right by a small post carrying the North Wales Path sign (ignore a minor path on the left here) to eventually run beside a ruined stone wall. Bear right through a gap in the wall (indicated by the NWP sign) and continue to a ladder stile beside a large gate, which lies at the end of a farm track. Follow the track which rises gradually up the hillside to pass beneath a line of power cables.

There are excellent views from here, both back towards the Aber Falls at the head of the valley and the northern outliers of the Carneddau which back it, and to your right across the valley to Foel Ganol and the Roman road, marked by pylons on the skyline. This road came up from the ford at Tal-y-Cafn to Bwlch-y-Ddeufaen, then across the foot of Drum, Foel Ganol and down into the valley to Abergwyngregyn. The Roman leader Suetonius Paulinus used this route in AD 61 to reach Anglesey in a bid to put an end to the Druid resistance. This was successfully completed in one bloody massacre on the shores of the Menai Strait, when the Druid priests were slaughtered and their sacred groves burned to the ground. The road continued in use throughout the Roman period and became the main link between the forts at Caernarfon and Chester.

The Romans were, however, not the first to use this route through the mountains. The numerous prehistoric remains which line it testify to its antiquity and indicate that it had been in use throughout the Iron Age, Bronze Age and Neolithic period. The oak woods on the far side of the valley are a reminder of the woods that would have covered much of Snowdonia until the clearances of the Middle Ages.

Continue along the track until you pass a narrow wood on the left and broad views open out across the Lafan Sands to Anglesey. Continue, to pass a corrugated iron sheep shelter on the left and pass through a gap in a ruined stone wall. Immediately, a path forks left (signed NWP) and the track bears right and descends to Abergwyngregyn (the track can be used to shorten the walk). Bear left off the track here and follow the path which, after passing through a small wood, keeps to the top of the hillside.

The vast expanse of the Lafan Sands was used for many years as part of the route to Holyhead and Ireland. This may seem strange to us today, but prior to the building of coach roads in the late eighteenth century, most travel was carried out either on foot or horseback and where possible the shortest distance was taken. With no bridge at

Aber Falls/Rhaeadr Fawr

Menai until the 1820s, the shortest route from Conwy was across the Lafan Sands to Beaumaris and then through the centre of Anglesey to Holyhead by another tidal crossing to Holy Island. A ferry ran from Beaumaris to the edge of the sands for the crossing of the Menai Strait at low tide—one of the reasons why Beaumaris was previously such an important town on the island.

3. Follow the track along the top of the hillside passing through a number of grazing fields for about 2 kilometres/1¼ miles. Immediately before a ladder stile, follow the track as it bends right and drops steeply down the field (the NWP continues ahead at this point). Lower down the track curves right to a gate. Go through the gate and bear left off the track keeping close to the stream in the trees to your left. Look for a stile at the bottom of the field to the right of a small stone cottage. After the stile, walk down the access road for about 50 metres or so before turning right through the centre of the field. Look for a ladder stile in the fence ahead beside a wooden gate. Cut through the next field aiming for a stile behind farm buildings. At the end of the outbuildings drop to a gate, which leads into the yard. Walk straight through the yard keeping the farmhouse on your left, to enter fields again by a gate. Follow a track which runs across the field before rising to a gate and ladder stile. Beyond the gate the track contours the hillside.

At a fork, keep left and drop to a group of houses. Look for a ladder stile immediately to the left of the last house, which leads into fields again. Walk directly through the field, contouring the hillside and go through an iron kissing gate in the far corner. Keep to the field edge in the following field and pass through a second kissing gate. Go ahead now following the obvious path and ignoring a ladder stile on the left adjacent to a house, which would take you into Abergwyngregyn. At the end of the path a kissing gate and steps take you into the lane. Turn right here and follow the lane back to the car park to complete the walk.

18. Llyn Crafnant & Llyn Geirionydd

Two lovely upland lakes

A popular circuit around two mountain- and forest-fringed lakes

Start: *Llyn Crafnant is reached by following the signed lane from Trefriw opposite the 'Fairy Falls Hotel'. Parking is available in a large, fee paying Forest Enterprise car park with toilets, just before the lake. Map reference: SH 757 618.*

Distance: *7.5 kilometres/4¾ miles.*

Duration: *Allow 2½-3 hours.*

Difficulty: *Easy-moderate. Footpaths are good throughout.*

Food and Drink: *Pubs and cafés in Trefriw and tearooms at Llyn Crafnant.*

Map: *OS 1: 50,000 Landranger 115 Snowdon; OS 1:25,000 Explorer/Outdoor Leisure OL 17 Snowdon.*

ENCIRCLED BY MOUNTAINS AND FORESTS, two beautiful lakes above the Conwy Valley form the perfect setting for a pretty and ever-popular circular walk.

The walk

1. Turn right, out of the car park and walk up the road to the lake.

This will be your first view of Llyn Crafnant and the beautiful valley that encloses it. The name Crafnant is possibly derived from the words craf, *which means 'wild garlic' and* nant, *a 'stream'. If this is the case, then the name Crafnant means: 'stream of wild garlic'.*

101

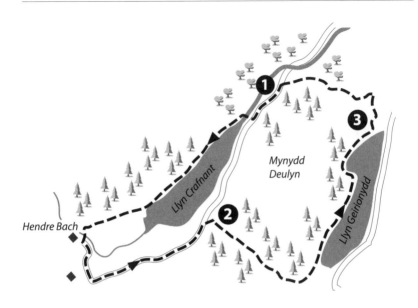

A column near the outflow of the lake records the gift made by Richard James of Dyffryn Aur to Llanrwst Parish Council in 1895, enabling them to take a water supply from the lake.

Turn right immediately before the lake, pass through a kissing gate, and follow a forest road which keeps close to the water's edge. Keep left at a fork in the track, about half way along the lake.

Beyond the lake, the track becomes rougher then rises gently. Just before the track crosses a bridge over a stream, turn left down the bank on a signed footpath. Follow the path down through young pines to cross a footbridge over the stream to join the access track to 'Hendre Bach', on the right. Turn left along the track and follow it to a tarmac lane. Turn left along the lane and continue for about 1 kilometre/¾ mile.

2. Immediately before a telephone box and small stone building, bear right onto a signed footpath to *'Geirionydd'*. Rise steadily to meet a path junction—turn right and follow the well-worn path up through woods.

At the top of the rise, go through a gap in the wall and a short drop brings you to a forestry road. Turn right down the hill for about 30 metres and immediately after a track on the left on the bend, turn left onto a narrow footpath. This path heads directly downhill crossing the forest road twice before you arrive at a T junction with fields below and ahead. Turn left along the track and where this bends right, turn left (ahead) over a stile. Walk through the following field with the waters of Llyn Geirionydd to the right. Enter the woods again and continue along the water's edge for about 1.5 kilometres / 1 mile.

Sadly, this beautiful lake has become a casualty of the local mining industry. Its waters have been poisoned by lead and other minerals seeping from nearby waste tips, and are almost sterile.

Llyn Crafnant

As you approach the end of the lake, leave the woods behind and follow the footpath ahead to a small stone barn on the right. Immediately after this, turn left along the access road to a house and after 10 metres or so, turn right at a waymarker. Walk up to a stone monument and look back for a fine view of Llyn Geirionydd and the steep hillside of Mynydd Deulyn.

The monument was erected in 1850 by Lord Willoughby d' Eresby of nearby Gwydir to commemorate the supposed birthplace of Taliesin, the famous sixth century bard. Numerous stories surround this mystical character but perhaps the best known is his association with King Maelgwyn Gwynedd. Maelgwyn, who ruled from 510-547, was the great-grandson of Cunedda, the powerful chieftain who came from one of the northern British kingdoms in the fifth century to rid Wales of Irish invaders and established the kingdom of Gwynedd. By the time of Maelgwyn the Irish threat had gone and he was able to use a period of peace and prosperity to indulge in a life of extravagance and luxury rare among his contemporaries.

He built a palace at Deganwy on a hilltop known today as The Vardre, which overlooks the mouth of Afon Conwy, but his lifestyle soon brought condemnation and he was declared to be one of the most 'sinful rulers' of his day by the monk Gildas, a sixth century chronicler and contemporary.

Despite his failings, Maelgwyn was a lover of music and poetry and harboured many musicians and bards at his court. On one occasion, his nephew Elffin came to visit and brought with him his bard, the great Taliesin. Maelgwyn's famous temper flared during the visit and the two parted enemies. Taliesin's parting gift to Maelgwyn was to foretell his death—'a creature would rise from Morfa Rhianedd *(the plain on which Llandudno now stands)* to punish him, its hair, its teeth and its eyes are yellow and this makes an end of Maelgwyn Gwynedd.'

Maelgwyn is said to have been so terrified that he locked himself into the church at Llanrhos but unable to resist his curiosity, he looked through the keyhole, saw the creature waiting and died on the spot.

This story, though fanciful, may have some elements of fact. Maelgwyn is known to have died in 547, possibly of the yellow plague which swept Europe during the mid-sixth century. With news of its progress through Britain, Maelgwyn may have anticipated his fate and retired to the nearby church to die.

The Taliesin Monument is also noted for its associations with the Eisteddfod organised by the bard Gwilym Cowlyd (real name William John Roberts), in the second half of the nineteenth century. He worked as a poet, printer and bookseller and published the works of a number of fellow poets. As a bard he was highly respected and won the Chair at the National Eisteddfod at Conwy in 1861. His high standards led him into disagreement with the rules, so together with an associate, he organised a rival Eisteddfod in 1863 under the name of 'Arwest Glan Geirionydd'. The location was here around the Taliesin monument for obvious reasons and for a while it rivalled the National Eisteddfod in popularity, attracting entries from all over Wales.

When Gwilym died in 1904 at the age of 76, the great driving force behind the event was gone. It was held for the last time in 1912.

3. Drop to a path directly behind the monument, bear right and keep to the right of a small group of conifers. Beyond the trees, follow the path down to cross a stone wall by a stile. Immediately after the stile, keep left at a fork and follow a rising path through young birch woods. After a second wall at a T junction a little further on turn left. Stay on the clear path eventually passing through an area of old mines. A stile now leads onto a forestry road. Keep right down the hill to return to the car park to complete the walk.

19. Capel Garmon & the Fairy Glen

Prehistoric burial chamber and dramatic river gorge

From Afon Conwy up to Capel Garmon and back via the Victorians' famous 'Fairy Glen'

Start: *There is limited parking in a layby in the minor lane immediately north of its junction with the A470 where it passes over Afon Conwy, about 1.5 kilometre/1 mile south of Betws-y-coed. Map reference: SH 797 546.*

Distance: *6.5 kilometres/4 miles.*

Duration: *Allow 2½ hours.*

Difficulty: *Moderate. A varied and fairly strenuous walk up to the village of Capel Garmon followed by a descent into the deep gorge cut by the Afon Conwy. Footpaths are good and easily followed throughout.*

Food and Drink: *White Horse Inn, Capel Garmon. Friendly bar. Restaurant and bar food. B&B accommodation. 01690 710271.*

Map: *OS 1: 50,000 Landranger 115 Snowdon; OS 1:25,000 Explorer/Outdoor Leisure OL 17 Snowdon.*

ANCIENT AND MODERN WELSH HISTORY come alive in this short but rewarding circuit. In a few short kilometres the walk spans several thousand years—from the well-preserved Neolithic burial chamber at Capel Garmon to the Victorian tourist honey-pot of the Fairy Glen.

The walk

1. Walk back to the A470 and turn left over the bridge. Take the path on the right immediately before the 'Fairy Glen Hotel'.

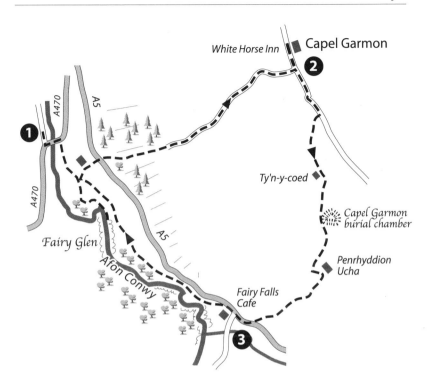

Continue until you come to the access path to Fairy Glen on the right. A small fee is payable by those who wish to make a visit. Return to this point to continue the walk.

Fairy Glen became popular and acquired its English name during the Victorian period, when new roads allowed nearby Betws-y-Coed to develop from a small hamlet on the Irish mail route, into a tourist destination in its own right. The Victorians revelled in the romantic landscape of the area and the walk to Fairy Glen became one of their most popular excursions.

Opposite the path to Fairy Glen, take the enclosed footpath on the left which rises beside a stone cottage ('Cwmanog Isaf'). Go through a gate behind the cottage and continue the climb to the A5. Cross the road and take the path directly opposite which passes through a gap in the wall. Climb steeply beside a stone

Neolithic burial chamber at Capel Garmon

wall at first, then zig-zag up through the trees until a forest road is reached and the angle eases considerably. Turn right along the road and follow this to the tiny village of Capel Garmon set amongst rolling farmland high above the Conwy Valley with stunning views west to Snowdonia's highest mountains.

Capel Garmon is a quiet, isolated village well off the beaten track and virtually unknown. It is worth the short detour into the village for the view from the church cemetery—one of the best mountain views in Wales. The White Horse is an excellent village pub, but at the time of writing is only open in the evening.

2. Return to the lane junction on the edge of the village but continue ahead instead of turning right. After about 600 metres the lane bends, and you pass the driveway to 'Maes y Garnedd' on the right. From here the lane rises gently and in about 100 metres there is a signed footpath and kissing gate on the right. Go through the gate and walk along the left-hand field edge. A kissing gate leads into a second field and the right of way continues straight ahead towards a small farm ('Ty'n-y-coed'). As you approach the farm bear left, as signed, to enter the farmyard by a gate. Walk up the access road past the farmhouse and where this bends sharp left, go right, down to a kissing gate and footpath sign which leads into a field on the left. Walk beside the fence on the right and about halfway along the field turn right through a gate. Bear diagonally-left across the field to the site of the burial chamber.

This is one of the best examples of a Neolithic burial chamber in the locality and also has one of the finest settings—backed by a panorama of Snowdonia's highest peaks. As with almost all such remains, the original mound which covered the site has been eroded but a line of stones enclosing the chamber mark its extremities. The remains consist of a triple chamber faced with drystone walling as well as large upright stones using a 'post and panel' technique. This has been extensively restored but original work can be seen in the lower courses of the eastern chamber. These were originally topped by large capstones but only one remains. In 1924 restoration work was carried out and steps taken to halt any further deterioration.

Leave the site by the gate and turn right to a kissing gate in the wall. Walk ahead for 50 metres or so, then bear half-left following the right of way over a small rocky rise, passing a fingerpost and dropping to a ruined stone wall (ignore a large field gate over to the right here). Go through the gap in the wall and make a gentle rise through trees to another small field. Go directly through this field to reach a rough farm track where there is another fingerpost.

Turn right along the track and follow it down the hill towards Penrhyddion Ucha, a small hill farm with a view of Cwm Penmachno directly ahead. About 150 metres before the farm, bear right onto a footpath diversion as indicated by a fingerpost. Walk down the field parallel to the fence on the right, to a stile by outbuildings on the left, which leads into a narrow lane.

Turn left up the lane and almost opposite the farm entrance, turn right through a gate into the yard of a smaller cottage / farm. Turn right immediately, then left by stone outbuildings and go through a gate. Go ahead through a small rough garden area crossing a stream to a ladder stile which leads into fields. Bear right down the field keeping to the right-hand edge and pass through a kissing gate on the right. Cross the stream and bear left through a small grazing field to a kissing gate in the wall which takes you into a campsite ('Rynys Camping Site'). Walk ahead until you are level with the house, then bear right down the access road to the lane. Turn left down the lane and follow this to the busy A5.

3. Turn right and walk along the road to the 'Conwy Falls Café and Restaurant'. (Take care on this section as there is no footpath and the road is often very busy.) Ignore the lane on the left here and about 200 metres beyond the café (just after the bend), bear left through a gap in the wall, which takes you onto a well defined path with Afon Conwy down to your left.

This pleasant path is all that remains of the old toll road built by the Capel Curig Turnpike Trust in the nineteenth century. It provided a link between an earlier toll road which came to Pentrefoelas from the east but then headed north to Llanrwst via Nebo and the road constructed by Lord Penrhyn between Bangor and Tŷ Hyll (the 'Ugly House'). It crossed Afon Conwy at Pont yr Afanc where the walk started, and continued through Betws-y-Coed, providing a London to Holyhead road which avoided all the problems of the coastal route via Conwy.

Stone embankments and buttresses can still be seen at various points along its length but it was still very narrow and steep gradients made it both difficult and dangerous for coaches. It became redundant in 1815 when Thomas Telford built what is now the A5. Telford took a line higher up the hillside which was less steep (never more than 1:22) but he records in his diary that the section above the Conwy Falls (directly above) was the most difficult of the entire route through the mountains.

Lower down, the path widens into a broader track lined with oak and beech trees, which would have clothed much of the valley during the Middle Ages. Follow the track back to the A470 and turn left to complete the walk.

20. Llyn Elsi

High forest lake and mountain views

Up through dappled woodland to Llyn Elsi, a pine-fringed
upland reservoir above Betws-y-Coed

Start: *There are a number of car parks as well as street parking
available in Betws-y-Coed. Begin the walk at the old stone bridge
carrying the B5106 over Afon Llugwy, opposite the 'Pont-y-Pair
Hotel'. Map reference: SH 792 568.*

Distance: *5.5 or 7.5 kilometres/3½ or 4¾ miles.*

Duration: *Allow 2-3 hours.*

Difficulty: *Moderate. Paths are good throughout, particularly in the
forest areas. Some moderate ascents.*

Food and Drink: *Numerous pubs, restaurants, cafés and fish and
chip shop in Betws-y-Coed. 'Royal Oak Hotel'. 01690 710219.*

Map: *OS 1: 50,000 Landranger 115 Snowdon; OS 1:25,000
Explorer/Outdoor Leisure OL 17 Snowdon.*

ONE OF THE BEST WALKS FROM BETWYS-Y-COED, this varied circuit
crosses the Afon Llugwy by the curious Miners' Bridge before
ascending gently through the forest to circle upland Llyn Elsi.

The walk

1. Cross the river and take the first road on the left immediately
after the bridge. After about 30 metres there is a pay and display
car park on your right; bear left here and follow the riverside
footpath.

The first section of the path is an 'all ability path' using a
raised wooden walkway and then a surfaced path. This leads to
picnic tables close to the river (about 350 metres) after which the
paths swings right. Go ahead at this point off the surfaced path

111

and past the picnic tables to locate a ladder stile hidden behind rocks immediately adjacent to the river. Over the stile, the path continues across fields beside the river.

Afon Llugwy drains the eastern mountains of northern Snowdonia, including much of the Ogwen valley and Dyffryn Mymbyr. In its journey east to join the Conwy it has carved the only breach in a high plateau area and has thus been used as a major communication route for centuries. Betws-y-Coed owes its existence to the use of this route as part of the London to Holyhead road during the eighteenth century.

After the fields, enter woods again and continue ahead on the riverside path to a large wooden footbridge spanning the river known as the 'Miner's Bridge'.

The name of this bridge recalls the occupation of many of the locals when lead mining was carried out in the hills to the north during the nineteenth century. The original bridge provided a short cut for miners living at Pentre Du on the south side of the river, thus saving them the mile and a half walk via the old bridge at Betws-y-Coed.

2. Cross the bridge and climb the steps out of the rocky bed of the river. Take the path ahead which shortly brings you to the A5. Cross the road and take the access road opposite, turning right almost immediately. A short rise brings you to a parking/turning area behind a row of stone cottages.

Turn left off the road here and follow the path beside the stream on your left. The path soon bears right just before a small waterfall and makes a rise to a T junction with a prominent forestry road. Turn left and follow the road over the stream passing a house on the right. Ignore the forest road that swings right immediately before the house; instead, continue ahead and about 150 metres beyond the house, look for a narrow but well used footpath on the right. This weaves through the woods to emerge in a small field (over a stile) with spoil heaps from disused mine workings on your right. Walk ahead through the field and cross a stile in the lower right-hand corner. Turn right, then immediately left, passing the ruins of mine buildings on the right, to cross a stream.

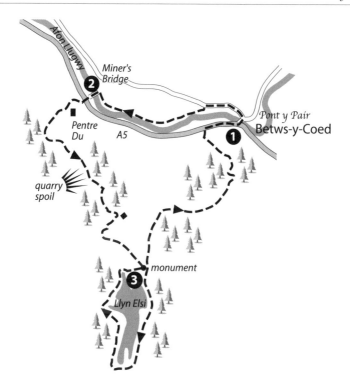

These spoil heaps and deserted buildings are the remains of Hafod-las slate quarry, which operated during the last century. It was worked by the men of Pentre Du and the now deserted village of Rhiwddolion, situated on the plateau above the quarry.

At the top of the rise bear left by the fence and in about 75 metres, turn right at a footpath T junction. Follow the prominent path, which soon bends sharp left by a deep quarry on the right, to a gate and ladder stile over the wall. Follow the path up through a small field to an old barn. Climb over the stile immediately before the barn, turn right and continue the climb along a farm track / path with views of the valley and the eastern Carneddau to the right.

At the top of the rise turn sharp left onto a path which skirts the conifer plantations to your right. (This is shortly before a stone farmhouse and a gravel access road.) A little further on, a stile on the right takes you into the trees. Follow the obvious footpath to a forestry road and cross over taking the footpath ahead to a T junction with a good footpath. Turn left here and follow the path to the memorial stone overlooking Llyn Elsi (pictured below).

This elevated lake surrounded by woods makes a fine foreground for panoramic views of Snowdonia's highest summits, but not Snowdon itself, which is hidden behind Moel Siabod, the most prominent peak in the view. To the right, the bulky Glyder ridge can be seen, with Tryfan's serrated outline peeping over the shoulder of Galt yr Ogof. Across the Ogwen valley rise the rounded and often snow covered slopes of the Carneddau.

Llyn Elsi

The memorial stone was erected to commemorate the opening of a new water supply from Llyn Elsi, by Betws-y-Coed Urban District Council in 1914.

To return to Betws-y-Coed from here continue from point 3 (below). Alternatively, you can walk around the lake first.

A good footpath leads away from the memorial along the left-hand side of the lake, soon joining a forest track. Bear right here and follow the track that continues to the far end of the lake. Beyond the dam the track swings right, then bends left to begin a descent into the lower woods. Look for a narrow footpath here on the right. Turn right and follow the path as it rises then bends rightwards around the lake.

Soon the water comes into view again down to the right and about halfway along the lake turn right onto an obvious footpath which drops down the bank to run close to the water's edge. Immediately before the dam, turn left up wooden steps and follow the path as it curves right to cross the outflow by a wooden footbridge. Turn right here and rise to the memorial again.

3. Stand with the memorial to your back and, facing the path which you have just used, take the next well worn footpath in a clockwise direction (at about 2 o'clock and almost due north).

At a junction of forest tracks, go ahead across the first track, then bear right almost immediately along a good forest path. Follow this through the woods to cross over a second forest road about half way down the hillside.

The path begins to steepen now and there are a few tantalising glimpses of what at one time must have been superb views down to Betws-y-Coed and up the valley to Llanrwst. Unfortunately the tree cover now obscures much of the view.

Almost at the A5 and within earshot of the traffic, turn left at a T junction with a forest track and after about 30 metres turn right onto a narrow footpath, which soon brings you to the road. Turn right now and walk back through Betws-y-Coed to complete the walk.

21. Sychnant Pass
Wide views above the Sychnant Pass

Through high pastures with dramatic views to the coast on one of the finest sections of the North Wales Path

Start: *There is parking for a number of cars at the top of the Sychnant Pass. Map reference: SH 750 770. If this is full, there is further parking space on the Conwy side of the pass. Map reference: SH 756768.*

Distance: *9 or 11 kilometres/5½ or 6¾ miles.*

Duration: *Allow 3-3½ hours.*

Difficulty: *Moderate. A fairly strenuous walk through the high pastures above the Sychnant Pass. Footpaths are excellent throughout.*

Food and Drink: *Two pubs offer lunchtime and evening food at Capelulo. The Fairy Glen. Restaurant and bar food, home cooked meals, B&B accommodation, families welcome. 01492 623107. Y Dwygyfylchi Hotel, B&B accommodation. 01492 623395.*

Map: *OS 1: 50,000 Landranger 115 Snowdon; OS 1:25,000 Explorer/Outdoor Leisure OL 17 Snowdon.*

HIGH ABOVE THE SYCHNANT PASS, this lovely upland circuit promises broad views spanning the coast from Anglesey in the west to the Great Orme on the North Wales coast.

The walk

1. Cross the road and go through the large gate between stone pillars almost opposite ('Pensychnant Nature Reserve and Farm'). Follow a good footpath with woods on the left for about 200 metres before turning sharp right at a T junction as indicated by the North Wales Path (NWP) sign. Rise gently up the hillside soon swinging leftwards to follow the broad grassy path under power

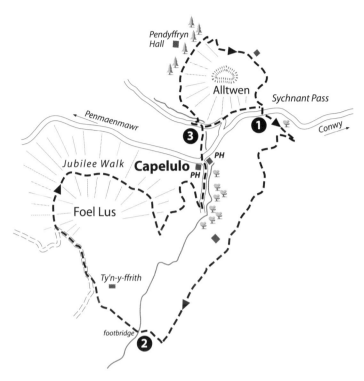

cables. About 200 metres after the cables, bear right with the main footpath. Follow this path passing under the power cables again and where you pass beneath the cables for the third time keep directly ahead (ignoring a prominent right turn). Follow this path for almost 1 kilometre / ¾ mile.

Climb a ladder stile over the wall beside a gate and follow the track ahead which curves in from the left. Beyond a cottage down to the right, the track curves leftwards, then forks—keep right here (NWP) passing under overhead cables again and soon walking beside a stone wall on the right. Stay beside the wall until it curves away to the right. Take the obvious path straight ahead.

Follow the obvious path ahead over open moors to reach an area of wall-enclosed fields ahead. Turn right (NWP) beside the wall, then bear half-left at the corner to a footbridge over a stream.

2. Cross the stream and take the good footpath ahead towards a farm (Ty'n-y-ffrith). Just before the farm there is a fork in the path where the North Wales Path bears left. Bear right here to a ladder stile over the wall. Beyond the stile the footpath bears half-left to a little bwlch or saddle where there is a junction of unsurfaced roads. Follow the road ahead down the hill.

Continue down the road to a sharp left-hand bend. Turn right on the bend between two large stone pillars, which mark the beginning of a contouring footpath.

This path is known as Jubilee Walk and was opened in 1888 to commemorate Queen Victoria's Jubilee the previous year. It follows the 250 metre contour and gives dramatic views into the valley of Penmaenmawr and Dwygyfylchi, as well as across the bay to the Great Orme and Penmon Point on Anglesey.

This sheltered valley is enclosed by the two great headlands of Penmaenbach and Penmaenmawr, which caused travellers so much trouble in the days before the coast road was built. During the seventeenth and eighteenth centuries, the route from Chester to Holyhead on Anglesey was known as the 'Great Irish Road' and came to Conwy via Denbigh—this however, was its most notorious section. Coaches were often taken along the beach at low tide while passengers proceeded on foot or horseback over the Sychnant Pass and the precarious route over Penmaenmawr. There was then a dangerous crossing of the Lafan Sands to the ferry at Beaumaris.

The Jubilee Walk ends on the far side of Foel Lus overlooking Capelulo and the Sychnant Pass (there is also a bench and power cables overhead here). Continue straight ahead and take the first narrow path on the left in 50 metres or so, which drops diagonally down the hillside to a stream. Cross the stream and keep straight ahead on a contouring footpath across grassy slopes overlooking Capelulo. At a T junction with a broad grass track turn left down the hillside passing a small cottage on the left (ignore signed footpaths on the left). Beyond the cottage, the

On the North Wales Path above Capelulo

track enters woods and drops to a gate. Go through the gate and turn sharp left along a lane. Follow this into Capelulo.

Although Capelulo is an ancient settlement, the village in its present form came into being when the Sychnant Pass road was opened in 1772. This road linked Conwy to Holyhead and avoided the long and strenuous climb to Bwlch-y-Ddeufaen above Rowen, or a dangerous crossing of the sands below the headland of Penmaenbach. For a while it formed part of the Irish mail road which came via Denbigh and the ferry at Conwy. Three inns were opened to provide lodgings and refreshment for those ascending or descending the pass.

This trade came to a sudden end in 1825 when Thomas Telford built a bridge at Conwy and a new road along the coast (the old A55). Capelulo returned to its former seclusion until the 1870s when Victorian tourists discovered the area and came to admire its dramatic scenery. Excursions from the nearby growing resort of Llandudno were popular around the turn of the century.

There are two pubs here—'The Fairy Glen' and 'Y Dwygyfylchi'. Between the pubs on the opposite side of the road there is an enclosed footpath; follow this path to a second road. For a shorter round turn right here, walk up the lane and at the bend, take the rising footpath straight ahead up the valley back to the car park (1 kilometre / ¾ mile).

3. Alternatively, for a longer walk incorporating the woods of Pendyffryn Hall (an additional 2.5 kilometres / 1¼ miles), turn left and walk down the lane to a bridge over the stream on the right. Cross the bridge turning right immediately and walk in front of stone cottages. At the end of the terrace take a signed footpath on the left which passes behind the cottages, then bears right up steps into the woods.

Follow a contouring path to a kissing gate, then go ahead through the trees beside the fence until the path splits and the hall is visible to the left (shortly before caravans ahead). Bear right here and follow the path as it rises to a ladder stile.

Climb over the stile and continue on the obvious path ignoring a footpath on the right which cuts directly up the hillside. A little further on, the path narrows and there is a fork; keep right here and zig-zag up the hillside.

At the top of the slope turn right and follow a broad grassy footpath beside a wall-enclosed field on the left. At the end of the wall, walk ahead to meet a path at a T junction. Bear left here to pass a small pool (often dry in the summer) keeping to the left of the water to join a broad path that runs beside the wall on the left. Join a farm access road and bear right. Follow this to a finger post carrying the NWP signs. Turn right here, rise over a bank and descend to join the track again, which you should now follow back to the Sychnant Pass to complete the walk.

Northeast Wales

22. Llanelidan

Across rolling parkland with wide views

A lovely walk through parkland and across wooded hills

Start: *Park on the road in Llanelidan or by the village hall just past the church and pub. Map reference SJ 110 505.*

Distance: *8 kilometres/5 miles.*

Duration: *Allow 2½-3 hours.*

Difficulty: *Moderate. Gentle walking through the estate of Nantclwyd Hall followed by rolling farmland.*

Food and Drink: *Leyland Arms, Llanelidan. Good food, B & B accommodation. 01824 750822.*

Map: *OS 1: 50,000 Landranger 116 Denbigh & Colwyn Bay; OS 1:25,000 Explorer 264 Vale of Clwyd.*

LLANELIDAN'S 15TH CENTURY CHURCH with its pretty double bellcote, village hall, handsome stone pub and cricket green form an attractive group, complementing the nearby Nantclwyd Hall estate.

The walk

1. From the village hall turn left and walk along the road passing the church and pub. In about 40 metres, and immediately after the road crosses a stream, turn right onto a signed footpath alongside the stream. Walk past the cricket pavilion and bear half-left away from the stream across the field to a stile in the middle of a wooden fence. Cross the stile and continue ahead to another smaller stream—aiming for the stump of a felled oak in the hedge. Cross the stream by a large stone slab to the right of the stump, then bear right and climb diagonally up the field to a footpath waymarker and a stile onto the road. Turn right and walk along road for around 400 metres to an attractive cluster of old farm buildings on the right. Don't turn right onto the signed right of way down the driveway, but cross a stile to the left of the drive entrance, following a waymarked footpath through trees and into a field.

Walk ahead towards a clump of pines on a hillock, with the farmhouse on the right. Walk to the left of the hillock then downhill towards a lake, making for a stile in the far corner of the field by weeping willows at the far end of the lake. Cross the stile onto the road.

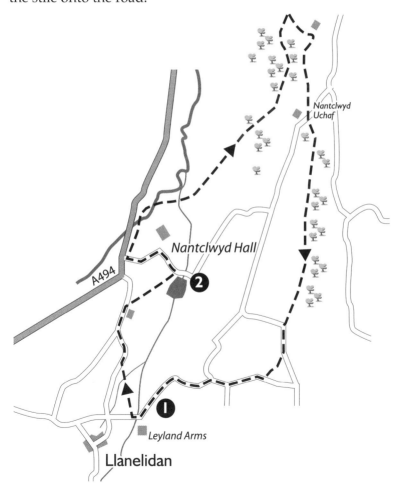

The lake and the surrounding wetland attract waterfowl, particularly in winter—black and white tufted duck and Canada geese are common.

2. Turn left and walk along the lane to the main road.

The grand country house over the hedge to the right is Nantclwyd Hall. The gardens have been elaborately restored, and feature stone gazebos, ornamental bridges and sculptures.

At the main road (A494) turn right and walk along a broad grassy verge for roughly 400 metres. Just beyond a stone bridge on the right and opposite the lane to 'Clocaenog', turn right onto a signed footpath through the hedge. This crosses the course of the old road and goes into the woodland ahead. Walk through the woodland for about 60 metres, bearing left on a narrow path that leads onto the manicured lawns of Nantclwyd Hall. Walk ahead with the river on the right, crossing the drive to the house (which passes over an ornate bridge on the right) and continue ahead to a large gate in the fence.

There are superb views of the mansion as you look down the driveway. The oldest part dates from the seventeenth century but it was extended and altered in the eighteenth and nineteenth centuries. In the 1950s and '60s it was elaborately remodelled by Sir Clough Williams-Ellis, the architect famous for the design of Porthmeirion.

Go through the gate or climb the wooden bars in the fence beside it and walk along the riverside to a pretty wooden footbridge. Cross the footbridge and walk diagonally-left across open grassland.

There are more good views to the right of the mansion with the lake in front. Colourful dragonflies and more slender-bodied damselflies dart across the edges or rest in the vegetation at the lake edge in summer.

Continue to a large gate and concrete bridge over a stream. Cross the bridge then climb diagonally-left across parkland. Walk uphill through dotted trees between a large fenced copse on the left and the main woodland on the hilltop to the right.

Crossing the footbridge near Nant Clwyd Hall

Continue contouring along the hillside parallel to the wood on the right. Pass a second smaller fenced copse on the left. At the far corner of the copse, turn right and walk to a gate and stile leading into the woodland.

Follow a narrow path leading half-left uphill through the trees.

The strong smell of wild garlic, with its dark green leaves and white flowers, fills the woodland in early spring, and is followed by a carpet of bluebells in May.

At the top of the wood go through a gate into a field and go ahead along a track to a large gate. Go through the gate into the next field and keep ahead until the Clwydian Range comes into view along with farm buildings ahead. Turn left and walk across the field to another wood—there is no longer a fence across the field but two large boundary trees roughly show the way.

There are good views of the Clwydian hills on the right as you walk across the field.

125

Go through the gate into woods and follow the footpath ahead (can sometimes be a bit overgrown in summer). This soon bears left through the woodland. Continue on the path to the woodland edge beside two ruined cottages. Cross a stile in the fence ahead beside a corrugated iron barn, then walk straight ahead for 75-100 metres or so to the end of the high hedge on the right. Turn right here along a rutted and sometimes muddy farm track that swings rightwards back towards the woods. The track weaves between scrubby bushes and becomes better established to eventually run alongside a stone wall with woodland on the right. Continue downhill to a gate and stile with a cottage on the left. Cross the stile and bear right along a track.

Walk along the track for about 500 metres eventually, leaving the woods. Cross a stile next to gate into a field on the right and walk diagonally-left across the field to a stile leading into a lane. Walk along the lane for about 50 metres then, just before the drive to a house on the right ('Nant Clwyd Uchaf'), cross a stile on the

Nantclwyd Hall

left into a field and walk ahead along the right-hand field edge, with woodland on the right.

Part way down the field, cross a stile on the right into woodland. Follow a meandering path through the woodland for about 150 metres to a gate leading into a field on the far side. Go through the gate and follow the left-hand field edge, keeping woodland on the left. Cross two large fields separated by a stile.

In the corner of the second field cross a stile under trees and cut directly across the following field, just to the left of centre, to a stile in the far corner. Turn left immediately over another stile into woodland and follow the path to the right, continuing in the same direction as before along the woodland edge. The path is difficult to find in places and may get overgrown in summer.

Wildflowers flourish on this grassy limestone bank at the woodland edge. In spring cowslips abound; look also for the spikes of early purple orchids.

Stay close to the woodland edge with fields to the right. Count the fields to your right. At the far fence of the second field bear right past the fence corner and then go ahead through trees to find a stile in the fence ahead beneath high hawthorn bushes. This takes you back into fields. Walk ahead along the field edge with thinning woodland on the left. Continue in the same direction, going through an old gateway in the hedge. Continue across the next field with the hedgerow on the right to a stile leading into the lane.

Turn right along the lane and at a T junction in a few metres turn left. Walk up the lane until you come to a pretty stone chapel on the left at the top of the rise. Just opposite the cottage attached to the chapel turn right and cross a stile into the field. Bear left across the field down to a stile in the hedgerow below. Turn right and walk down the road for 1km/¾ mile back to Llanelidan to complete the walk.

23. Cyffylliog
In the folds of the upper Clywedog

A delightful walk in unspoilt countryside among the tree clad
hills of the Clwyedog valley

Start: *There is limited roadside parking in Cyffylliog by the bridge.
Map reference SJ 060 578.*

Distance: *8 kilometres/5 miles.*

Duration: *Allow 2½ hours.*

Difficulty: *Moderate. A steady ascent out of the Clywedog valley.*

Food and Drink: *Red Lion Hotel, Cyffylliog. Food and
accommodation. 01824 710664.*

Map: *OS 1: 50,000 Landranger 116 Denbigh & Colwyn Bay; OS
1:25,000 Explorer 264 Vale of Clwyd.*

CYFFYLLIOG HAS A PEACEFUL AIR, hidden away in the valley
bottom. The simple terraced cottages, the inn and village school,
with its distinctive bell tower, are all attractive, but it is the
setting, high in the wooded Clywedog valley, threaded by narrow
wildflower-edged lanes that gives it its special quality.

The walk

1. This circuit is one of the waymarked walks in the Mynydd
Hiraethog and Denbigh Moors footpath network developed
by Conwy and Denbighshire Councils. It is waymarked with
special 'Mynydd Hiraethog' green circular discs which will be
seen throughout the walk.

From the bridge walk towards the Red Lion pub and take
the lane on the right signed to 'Nantglyn'. Walk along the lane
passing the church on the right.

Cyffylliog church is small with a simple stone belltower, set in a

128

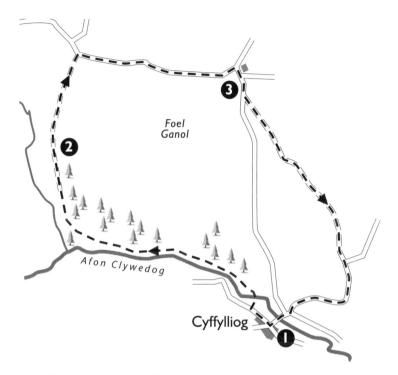

pretty churchyard with old gnarled yews. Next to the churchyard is a Georgian 'hearse house', a small stone building with large wooden doors, built to house the horse-drawn hearse.

Just past the church, take the waymarked footpath on the right immediately before a cottage. Follow the path over the river by a footbridge and bear left, walking with the river on your left.

The path leads to an old fording point on the river. Turn right along the waymarked riverside path, ignoring a bridge on the left. Follow this path through woodland with the river close by for approximately 1km / ¾ mile as it climbs gradually.

The Clywedog is fast flowing here, running over large slabs of stone and forming small waterfalls. An attractive mix of trees, including wild cherry and hazel grow on the steep banks which are carpeted with wild garlic in spring.

As you leave the woods, a gate leads onto an access track that curves right to a cottage out of view up to the right. Go ahead along the access track and where it begins to drop to cross a bridge bear right on a narrow woodland footpath.

This path leads along the right-hand side of the river and widens as it climbs up the hillside, with conifers on the right and a steep drop down to the river on the left. Continue on the path as it bears right away from the river. At the first path junction bear left downwards to a T junction. Turn right here and continue uphill on a good forest track.

2. Cross a gate or stile at the edge of the forestry plantation and follow the rising farm track as it climbs up, away from the river, with views back down into the valley and up onto the Denbigh Moors. Continue uphill to a lane.

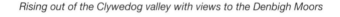

Rising out of the Clywedog valley with views to the Denbigh Moors

Turn right and continue along the lane for about 1.5 kilometres / 1 mile.

There are wide views to the left stretching out to the distant coast. In the foreground is the green rolling farmland of the Vale of Clwyd with the tower of Llanrhaeadr church just visible on a clear day and the northern Clwydians beyond. As you walk along the lane, views of the Clwydians change, as first Moel Arthur and then Moel Famau appear.

3. At a fork in the road, bear right, passing stone farm buildings on the left. Ignore a signed footpath on the right and continue ahead for 100 metres over a cattle grid, then take a clearly waymarked footpath immediately on the left. Follow this very clear grassy track for approximately 1.5 kilometres / 1 mile, gradually descending towards Cyffylliog.

The views are superb again with the Clocaenog Forest across the valley and rolling farmland with thick hedges and pockets of woodland all around.

At a gate and stile, cross over and continue ahead to the road. Turn right and walk along the road downhill. At the bottom of the hill turn right, cross the river on the main bridge and walk back into the village to complete the walk.

24. Penycloddiau & Moel Arthur

Two hillforts and everchanging panoramic views

Along the Clwydian Range to the earthen ramparts of two Iron Age hillforts and a lovely green lane around the lower slopes

Start: *Begin at the Llangwyfan Forest car park situated at the highest point of the lane which runs between Llangwyfan and Nannerch. Map reference: SJ 139 668.*

Distance: *7 or 10.5 kilometres/4¼ or 6½ miles.*

Duration: *Allow 3-3½ hours.*

Difficulty: *Moderate. A fairly strenuous route along the Clwydian Range with some steep climbs and descents. Paths are good throughout.*

Food and Drink: *No refreshments nearby.*

Map: *OS 1: 50,000 Landranger 116 Denbigh & Colwyn Bay; OS 1:25,000 Explorer 265 Clwydian Range.*

ONE OF THE BEST NATURAL CIRCUITS along the gently rounded tops of the Clwydian Range, this walk takes in the well-preserved ramparts of two Iron Age hillforts before looping back on a grassy track tracing the contours halfway down the slopes.

The walk

1. From the little car park follow the signed Offa's Dyke Path northwards into the plantations. Immediately you are presented with three forestry tracks—take the right-hand track for a few yards before bearing right onto a much narrower, though well used footpath which runs along the very edge of the trees.

Just before the earthworks which encircle the hilltop of Penycloddiau, turn right over a stile and follow the signed footpath to the summit cairn at the northern end of the enclosure.

The earthworks which encircle the summit form the largest Iron Age enclosure on the Clwydian Range. Over 20 hectares/50 acres lie within its triple banks, which are still remarkably well preserved. The earthworks are such a prominent feature of the hilltop that they have given it its name: Penycloddiau means 'head of the trenches'.

Thankfully, the nearby conifer plantations of the Llangwyfan Forest have stopped short of the summit enclosure, enabling the walker to enjoy extensive views over the Vale of Clwyd in fine weather. The distant peaks of Snowdonia are visible in clear conditions.

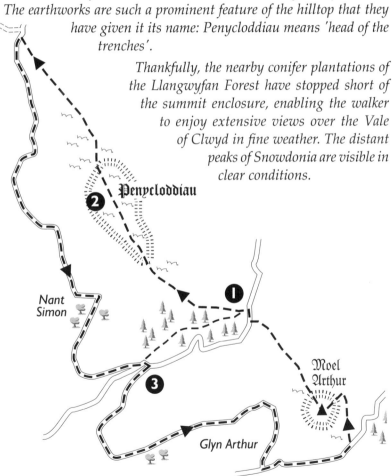

Penycloddiau

Nant Simon

Moel Arthur

Glyn Arthur

Approaching Penycloddiau with Moel Arthur behind

2. From the summit, follow the Offa's Dyke Path northwards out of the enclosure and across the open moors for almost 1 kilometre/¾ mile to a saddle crossed by unsurfaced green lanes.

Turn sharp left here onto a bridleway that contours the hillside for about 3.5 kilometres/2¼ miles.

If your walk along the exposed ridge was breezy you will be better able to enjoy the views westwards over the Vale of Clwyd from the relative shelter of this lower path.

As you leave the open deciduous woods at Nant Simon, where the path loops left to cross a stream, look for a path that bears left into conifers just before a gate. If you want to shorten the walk, follow this path back to the car park at point **1.** For a longer round, continue through the gate ahead and follow the track to a road.

3. Turn left along the road and when it bends left in about 150 metres, turn right, onto a bridleway again. After a gate near a house, the right of way continues as a narrower leafy path that contours the hillside for about 2 kilometres / 1¼ miles to join the hill road above Glyn Arthur.

Turn left along the road and walk up to the little car park at the top of the pass where you rejoin the Offa's Dyke Path.

Follow the signed Offa's Dyke Path on the left. This takes a rightward diagonal line aiming for a broad shoulder to the right of the summit of Moel Arthur. At the top of the rise a path on the left leads through heather to the exposed summit.

Like Penycloddiau, this hilltop is crowned by the earthworks of an Iron Age hillfort built over 2,500 years ago by the Celts who inhabited this part of Wales in the years before the Roman invasion.

At almost 450 metres /1,500 feet above sea level, the view is extensive and you are treated to a bird's-eye view of the Vale of Clwyd. Eastwards, you will be able to pick out the long arm of the Wirral peninsula with the hills between Beeston and Frodsham rising from the Cheshire Plain. To the south, the summit cone of Moel Famau, highest point on the Clwydian Range, rises above the surrounding moors, while the distant peaks of the Arans fill the skyline to the southwest.

From here, continue northwards to rejoin the main Offa's Dyke Path near a stile which leads into grazing fields. Follow the obvious path down the sloping fields to the road. Turn right here to the forest car park to complete the walk.

25. Moel Famau from Llangynhafal

Around the Clwydian Range's highest hill

Moel Famau's ruined Jubilee Tower and Moel-y-Gaer Iron Age
hillfort, with some of the finest panoramas in Northeast Wales

Start: *Just to the south of the village of Llangynhafal there is
a crossroads and about 200 metres south of this, on the lane to
Hirwaen, is a small layby with room for half a dozen or so cars.
Map reference: SJ 130 632.*

Distance: *9 kilometres/5½ miles.*

Duration: *Allow 2½-3 hours.*

Difficulty: *Moderate. A fairly strenuous walk on the steep western
slopes of Moel Famau high above the Vale of Clwyd. Footpaths are
generally good although a short section on the descent to Moel y
Gaer requires careful route finding.*

Food and Drink: *Golden Lion Inn, Llangynhafal. Restaurant and
bar food. Real ale. Real fires. Beer garden. B&B accommodation.
Closed Mondays. 01824 790451.*

Map: *OS 1: 50,000 Landranger 116 Denbigh & Colwyn Bay; OS
1:25,000 Explorer 265 Clwydian Range.*

APPROACHING THE SUMMIT OF MOEL FAMAU from the Vale of
Clwyd below, this unorthodox but pleasing loop also takes in the
heather-clad ramparts of Moel-y-Gaer Iron Age hillfort.

The walk

1. On the opposite side of the lane and a few yards back towards
Llangynhafal, take the signed path across a small field to enter
another lane. Turn right and follow the lane up to St Cynhafal's
parish church.

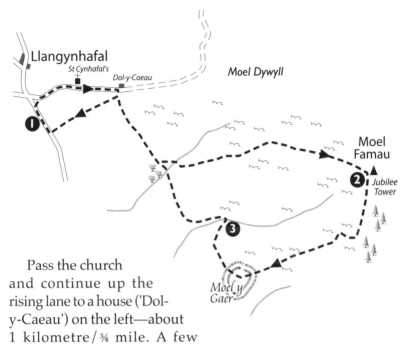

Pass the church and continue up the rising lane to a house ('Dol-y-Caeau') on the left—about 1 kilometre / ¾ mile. A few metres before the house, take the signed footpath on the right, which shortly leads onto the open hillside. The path contours above fields on the right with wide views across the Vale of Clwyd.

Continue, passing a striking Scots pine on the right at one point. A little beyond this, the path veers left, away from the walled fields on the right, and down into a small valley. Cross the stream and rise to a fork beside a fingerpost. Turn left here and follow the rising footpath up through summer bracken.

As the angle eases, the Jubilee Tower on the summit of Moel Famau comes into view. Continue on the obvious path which, as you approach the summit, curves left to join the Offa's Dyke Path at a T junction on the broad, whaleback ridge. Turn right and rise steeply up to the summit.

From the summit you can enjoy one of the finest panoramas in northeast Wales, particularly west across the Vale of Clwyd and the

Paths near the summit of Moel Famau

Denbigh Moors to the peaks of Snowdonia on the far horizon. North and south the views are along the switchback ridge of the Clwydian Range, while to the east lies the distant lowland of the Cheshire Plain, scarred by the Deeside and Merseyside industrial belts.

The ruined tower which crowns the highest point was built in 1810 to commemorate the 50th anniversary of the reign of King George III. It was originally designed in the Egyptian style to reach a height of 45 metres/150 feet, but the plans were never fully carried out and the structure collapsed in 1862 following a series of gales. Attempts to restore the tower for Queen Victoria's Golden Jubilee in 1887 were a failure and the modest structure which we now see is all that remains.

2. Take the Offa's Dyke Path south from the summit, following the signs for 'Bwlch Penbarra'. After the initial steep descent, the path levels, with conifer woods on the left.

The next section down to Moel y Gaer hillfort needs careful route finding. Continue until a small heathery rise on the left obscures the trees briefly and there is a bench on the right, inscribed 'Tower View, 1st April 2002, Tony Christopher'. A few metres further on, turn right onto a narrow footpath through the heather. This soon swings rightwards, back towards Moel Dywyll with its two summit cairns. At a point where the path becomes completely level, about 150 metres from the bench, look for a very narrow but visible path on the left. This path soon begins to descend and Moel y Gaer hillfort comes into view below.

Continue the descent down through bracken to a broad saddle, to enter the hilfort through a gap in the earthworks. In the centre of the enclosure a small stone cairn marks the highest point.

Like the other hillforts on the Clwydian Range, Moel y Gaer was constructed by Celtic tribes in the centuries before the Roman invasion and is unusual in being the only hillfort not situated on the main ridge itself. It is, however, easy to see why the site was chosen; with steep slopes on three sides, the only approach is from the east via this narrow connecting ridge, which would have been easy to defend.

Head northwest from the summit—towards the western end of the Vale of Clwyd where the hills meet the flat land—crossing the earthworks and descending to a well-hidden stile in the fence below. Cross the stile, and turn right, around a large area of gorse, then walk diagonally-right down the sloping field to where fences meet the stream in the bottom of the valley. At the bottom of the slope, before the fence, turn right, passing a waymarker post and continuing ahead to a second post. Turn sharp left here, as directed, between gorse on the left and the fence to the right, to reach a gate. Go through the gate and turn left, over the stream, to follow the footpath above a small, bracken filled valley down to the left.

3. After a slight rise the path swings right, to run beside walled fields on the left. Continue on this path, eventually joining the outward route just before the solitary Scots pine seen earlier.

Just before the path joins the lane, bear left, down to a gate. Go through the gate and follow a sunken bridleway down to the lane, where a right turn will take you back to the layby to complete the walk.

26. The Alyn gorge and Moel Famau

Along the river and over the hills

Riverside and woodland paths to Cilcain village and back over
Moel Famau and its eastern cwms

Start: *Begin the walk at Loggerheads Country Park. There is pay
and display parking at the Visitor Centre, along with café, and
toilets. Map reference: SJ 198 626. (An alternative start could be
made from the village of Cilcain. Begin at point 2.
Map reference: SJ 177 648.)*

Distance: *14 kilometres/8¾ miles.*

Duration: *Allow 3-4 hours.*

Difficulty: *Moderate. Good riverside, woodland and moorland paths
throughout. Steep ascents to Moel Famau.*

Food and Drink: *Café at Loggerheads Country Park. Also, 'We
Three Loggerheads' pub, Ruthin Road, opposite Country Park. Real
ales and home-cooked food. Restaurant. Riverside garden. Walkers
and children welcome. 01352 810337. 'White Horse Inn', Cilcain.
Real ale and real fires. Home cooked food. 01352 740142.*

Map: *OS 1: 50,000 Landranger 116 Denbigh & Colwyn Bay;
OS 1:25,000 Explorer 265 Clwydian Range.*

FROM ENCLOSED VALLEY BOTTOMS TO OPEN HILLTOPS, this walk
of complementary opposites offers wooded riverside paths
and breezy, open panoramas from the top of Moel Famau—the
Clwydian Range's highest summit.

The walk

1. From the car park, walk past the Loggerheads Visitor Centre, café, toilets and the small outdoor shop to cross the river by the footbridge. Turn left immediately, onto the path which runs beside the river. Stay on the main path and don't take any of the alternatives which bear left to run closer to the river.

At a gate, take the signed 'Leete Path' straight ahead.

This path follows the line of an old leat which can be seen quite clearly here and there. Built in 1823 by John Taylor of the Mold Mines Company, it was originally 2 metres and 1.5 metres deep and was designed to carry water to power waterwheel-driven mining machinery lower down the valley. It was abandoned in 1845.

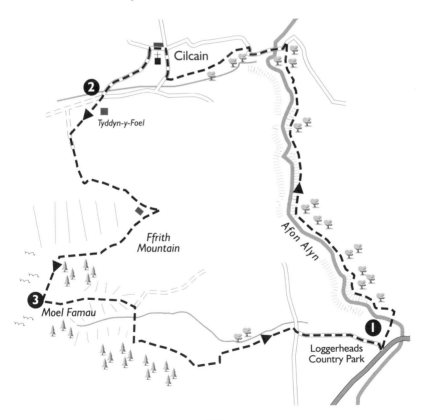

Stay on the 'Leete Path', ignoring other paths, and eventually joining the drive to 'Alyn Boarding Kennels'. Walk down the drive to a narrow lane and take the path opposite, through mature beech woods alive with colour in the spring and autumn.

The path is now high above the river and occasional views open out across the valley to Moel Famau, its smooth contours contrasting with the craggy outlines of this eastern side of Afon Alyn.

At one point you pass the half buried remains of a small bridge which once spanned the leat. Ignore the right fork here, continuing straight ahead, alongside the leat instead.

A little further on a footbridge takes you over Devil's Gorge—a legacy of the lead mining carried out all along the valley here. Fortunately operations ceased before too much damage was done to this beautiful valley.

Eventually the path swings right to join the road near the village of Pantymwyn. Turn left, walk down the hill and cross the little bridge, barely wide enough for modern vehicles to use. Ignore the signed bridleway soon after the bridge on the left; instead, stay on the rising lane and take the signed footpath to 'Pentre' ahead, at the top of the rise, where the lane bends sharp right. Follow an enclosed path at first, then enter fields by a stile. Keep left, along the field edge and, in a field or two, enter a field planted with young trees.

This is Coed y Felin, named after the nearby medieval water mill and was created by the Woodland Trust as part of the 'Woods on your doorstop' millennium project. At the top of the field on your right you will see a group of carved badgers.

Either turn right, up the field, past the carved badgers and then bear left along the top hedge to the lane, or continue a little further and turn left between two posts in the fence. Follow the path down a wooded bank to a path junction and turn right—ignoring a footbridge on the left—passing a small pool to reach the lane. Whichever route you take, turn right along the lane to the village of Cilcain.

Crossing the footbridge over Devil's Gorge, one of the old lead mines

Turn left at the 'White Horse Inn', and then left again immediately after the churchyard. Walk along the descending lane with its grand view of the curving hillside of Moel Famau.

2. After a short descent, the lane bends sharp left. Turn right onto a farm track here, then immediately left through a gate ('Tyddyn-y-Foel'). After about 20 metres, cross stone steps into fields on the right. Follow the right of way along field edges until a stile leads into a green lane near a junction of bridleways.

Turn left here and follow the green lane to a gate and stile. Immediately after this the track forks—take the path ahead, which is soon surfaced with large railway sleepers and curves left, to contour the hillside. Keep straight ahead through several fields, which can be boggy in wet conditions, to a gate near a cottage on the right. Pass the cottage and walk ahead down the rough access track towards a gate. Immediately before the gate, turn sharp right onto a good signed path which rises onto the rounded slopes of Ffrith Mountain.

Continue on the rising path which becomes less steep higher up, with views left into the long sweeping valleys which cut into Moel Famau's eastern slopes. At a junction of paths, turn left, up towards the summit, with conifer plantations to your left.

3. From the Jubilee Tower, walk almost due east, past the triangulation pillar, to cross a stile in the fence. Follow a descending path, which is steep at first, before the angle eases as you walk along the rounded crest of a broad ridge. Lower down, the path drops steeply again to join a farm track.

Turn right, along the track, crossing a stream with a deep valley on the right, with the wooded slopes of Moel Famau rising 200 metres/600 feet at its head. Turn left across the field and walk parallel to the stream until you reach a fingerpost (level with the edge of woods on the right), directing you half-right over a rounded ridge in the field to a second fingerpost beside oak trees further on. Walk straight ahead, soon with a fence on the left and another steep sided valley on the right, to cross a second stream.

Turn left on the signed path to a ladder stile in the fence corner, ignoring a stile into the trees on the right. Walk ahead by the fence, on a good path, to a stile on the left, and on into fields again. Bear right, through a small field to a stile, which leads into a short green lane. Turn left down a track and follow it as it bends right. Follow the track down to a lane.

Turn right along the lane, then left in a few metres, to return to Loggerheads Country Park to complete the walk.

27. Llantysilio Mountain
High above the Dee valley

A rolling ridge with wide views

Start: *Begin the walk at the tiny hamlet of Rhewl, 5 kilometres/ 3 miles west of Llangollen on the northern the banks of the River Dee/Afon Dyfrdwy. Park on a broad gravelled area opposite the little red brick chapel of Capel Hebron, in Rhewl. Map reference: SJ 183 449.*

Distance: *9.5 kilometres/6 miles.*

Duration: *Allow 4½-5 hours.*

Difficulty: *Medium-Hard. Long climb from the Dee valley, with undulating paths along the open tops. Several steep ascents and descents along the ridge. Return over sheep slopes, field paths and farm tracks.*

Food and Drink: *Sun Inn, Rhewl. Real ale, bar food, real fires, games room, beer garden. 01978 861043.*

Map: *OS 1: 50,000 Landranger 116 Denbigh & Colwyn Bay, and 125 Bala & Lake Vyrnwy; OS 1:25,000 Explorer 256 Wrexham & Llangollen.*

FOR A SENSE OF SPACE AND PANORAMIC VIEWS, the treeless whalebacks of Llantysilio Mountain are hard to beat. This circuit climbs from the lush Dee Valley up through woodland and pasture to the slate quarries and heather moorland of the tops.

The walk

1. Cross the road and follow the narrow lane which rises beside the chapel. Within 50 metres, bear right onto a short track with cottages on the right. A kissing gate behind the cottages leads onto a footpath which runs beside a stream. Fifty metres later, cross the stream on a narrow footbridge. Walk straight ahead, away from the stream, up the slope on a zig-zagging path that rises through the trees.

At the top of the bank, ignore a stile and path to the right; instead, bear left along the contours of the slope on a narrow path beneath the trees. The path continues along the top edge of a conifer plantation, now with the fence on your left, to emerge through a gap in the fence into a sloping grazing field. Bear uphill to the right, to a large metal gate at the top of a track rising from the left.

Immediately through the gate, turn left, uphill, on a waymarked farm track. Climb over a stile beside a second gate, and bear right, up the bank, to follow the waymarked right of way uphill alongside a sloping pine wood.

At the far end of the trees, a narrow footgate leads onto

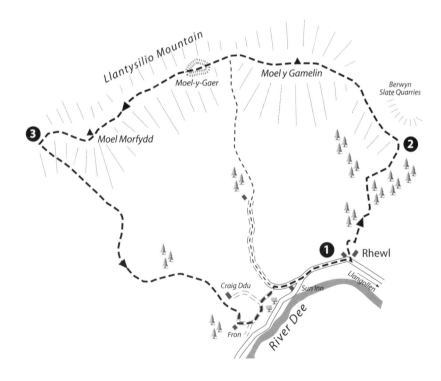

bracken-clad slopes; fine views of the Dee Valley open out below. Continue uphill, beside the fence, and then turn left along a broad grassy track.

Thirty metres later, turn right over a waymarked stile and rise diagonally right, up the hillside on a curving, grassy path. Follow the path as it rises alongside the pine wood, with gorse-clad slopes up to the left. When the wood ends, continue uphill on the clear grassy path over the moors.

As you break out onto the open moors, you increasingly benefit from the height gained. Below, the River Dee meanders through the lovely Glyndyfrdwy, surrounded by neat, sheep-grazed fields and small woods that rise gracefully to the heather-clad slopes of Llantysilio Mountain.

It was in this beautiful valley that Owain Glyndŵr lived until his rise to fame as the fifteenth century Welsh rebel leader and folk hero. Surprisingly, his journey to fame was triggered by a relatively minor incident—a quarrel over a small plot of land with his neighbour, Lord Grey of Ruthin. Grey it seems, was a royal favourite and managed to get Glyndŵr branded a traitor.

At a time of unrest—with much of Wales suspicious of the new king, Henry IV, who had obtained the crown by usurping Richard II—and in the face of such apparent injustice, Glyndŵr's countrymen were quick to support him, proclaiming him 'Prince of Wales'.

With his men behind him, he embarked on a series of raids and skirmishes which included the burning of both St Asaph Cathedral and the Ruthin estate of Lord Grey. During this campaign, his ability to disappear into the hills with his armies and appear again in another location with such speed gave rise to the belief that he possessed magical powers. Henry tried to suppress the uprising but Glyndŵr had gained the support of the powerful Sir Edmund Mortimer, Earl of Northumberland who was soon to become his son-in-law.

After failing to take the King's castles at Caernarfon and Harlech in 1401, he won a decisive battle on the slopes of Plynlymon and in 1404 managed to bribe a mutinous garrison into surrendering Harlech

Moel y Gamelin from the Berwyn Slate Quarries

Castle. He now had a headquarters and moved his entire family into the safety of the castle where they remained for four years.

Glyndŵr almost achieved his dream of a separate Welsh kingdom before his fortunes changed. Harlech fell, his supporters quickly left his side and by 1409, just nine years after his quarrel with Lord Grey, it was all over. He lived as an outlaw for many years, refusing a pardon from Henry V, and died in obscurity at an unknown location in the hills.

2. Just below the distinctive spoil heaps of the Berwyn Slate Quarries, turn left and follow a good path towards Moel y Gamelin, with the slate tips rising immediately to your right. Cross a boggy stream and continue, straight ahead through the heather and bilberries, on a steadily rising path to the summit of Moel y Gamelin.

From here on a clear day the panorama is one of the most extensive in northeast Wales. To the north, the Vale of Clwyd is laid out like a vast *green carpet, bordered to the east by the shapely, sheep grazed slopes of the Clwydian Range and on the west by the flat uplands of the Denbigh Moors. Further west, the pointed tops of Snowdonia are visible, while to the south the Berwyns rise above the Dee Valley. To the west, the view is dominated by the pale limestone crags of Eglwyseg Mountain, which rise steeply above the Vale of Llangollen.*

From the summit cairn, a steep descent to the west takes you to a saddle crossed by several tracks, including the long-distance Clwydian Way.

To shorten your walk, turn left here onto a broad track, then fork right, on the lower path (*not* the upper, left-hand Clwydian Way) and follow the bridleway across the slopes above a wood, to join a lane by Ty'n-y-mynydd. Follow the lane on downhill to the Sun Inn at Rhewl.

The main route, however, continues along the ridge, rising to the low ramparts of the Iron Age hillfort on Moel-y-Gaer. From here, the well-used path undulates across the rounded slopes, before snaking uphill again to the white-painted concrete Ordnance Survey triangulation pillar on the summit of Moel Morfydd. Continue west from Moel Morfydd and make a further steep descent.

Where the path levels out at the bottom of the slope, two tracks merge in a triangle of paths; turn sharp left here to join a prominent track which contours the hillside below the summit.

Around a kilometre later, the now grassy track levels out and bends sharply downhill to the right; continue straight ahead here on a slightly narrower, curving, grassy path, with Castell Dinas Bran soon clear on its hill ahead. At a sheep fence, turn right and follow the wire downslope to the field corner. Turn left over the stile, and then bear right, downhill again. Continue past a zig-zag in the fenceline, keeping the fence on your right. At the bottom of the slope, look for a fourway wooden fingerpost beside a gate at the junction of four fences. One finger points diagonally left across the sheep slopes. Head over the crest of the hill; roughly 200 metres to the right of the small conifer wood ahead, there is a waymarked stile at a corner of the fence.

3. Once over the stile, cross a boggy stream and climb over a second stile. Turn immediately left here, downhill on a waymarked path through the bracken. It drops downhill, now with the stream on your left, before skirting the top edge of the wood. Beyond the wood, the path continues downhill alongside the fence and tumbled drystone wall.

Just beyond the working farm below Craig Ddu, drop down to join a broad farm track. Turn right, along the track. Roughly 60 metres later, turn left over a stile, and drop down the field to an overgrown track that follows the fenceline down to the right. At the bottom of the field, turn left over a waymarked stile, then right, over another stile. A short path leads to a grassy access drive to nearby Fron cottage. Turn left down the drive, which is a 'permissive path'.

The drive curves above a wood, then kinks left to join a farm access track. Turn right here, along the track, and after passing over a stream, rise to a T junction. Turn right, downhill, along the lane to the Sun Inn at Rhewl, a tiny but delightful old drovers' inn and a welcome pint. From the Sun Inn, continue along the lane back to point **1.** at Rhewl to complete the walk.

28. Castell Dinas Bran & Trevor Rocks

Ruined castle and limestone cliffs

Up to ruined Castell Dinas Bran and along the dramatic limestone escarpment beyond Trevor Rocks, with magnificent views

Start: *Begin the walk at Llangollen's main, fee paying car park situated in Market Street (just off Castle Street) which leads down to the bridge. Map reference: SJ 215 420.*

Distance: *8 kilometres/5 miles.*

Duration: *Allow 3-3½ hours.*

Difficulty: *Moderate-strenuous. A fairly strenuous walk with a steep climb to Castell Dinas Bran and a high level walk along Trevor Rocks. Good paths over Dinas Bran and Trevor Rocks and field paths in the return to Llangollen. A section of the descent from Trevor Rocks involves a short scramble over a rock step that can be slippery in wet conditions, and a narrow path across scree.*

Food and Drink: *Numerous pubs, wine bars, restaurants, cafés, teashops and takeaways in Llangollen.*

Map: *OS 1: 50,000 Landranger 117 Chester & Wrexham; OS 1:25,000 Explorer 256 Wrexham & Llangollen.*

THE CONTRAST BETWEEN THE JAGGED LIMESTONE ESCARPMENT above Llangollen and the smooth sweeping contours to the west make this a fascinating and visually striking circuit. This is a landscape full of drama and history.

The walk

1. Turn right out of the car park, and at the end of the road turn left down Castle Street, to cross over the old Dee bridge.

This ancient bridge has spanned the river for over seven centuries and is thought to have been built during the reign of Henry I, and later widened by John Trevor, Bishop of St Asaph, in 1345. It seems likely that the town grew around this crossing although Llangollen's present size and form is mainly due to a short period of prosperity from the wool trade which flourished here for a while.

Today tourism keeps the local economy alive. One of the town's main attractions is the world famous International Eisteddfod. Originally started by a group of enthusiasts on a much smaller scale, it has expanded to become one of Wales' major events. During the festival, music groups and enthusiasts from around the world descend on the town until its tiny streets are almost swamped. Later these crowds will be housed in one of the largest marquees in the world specially designed for the event.

This is not the only Eisteddfod in Wales, nor was it the first. They have been held in Wales at least since the Middle Ages and before that similar gatherings at which bardic contests took place would always have been a part of Welsh culture. The word itself means simply 'to sit' and is taken from the verb 'eistedd'. Thus, an Eisteddfod is simply a sitting or 'gathering'.

Another event which draws in both spectators and participants from around the country is the canoeing championships, which use the fast flowing waters of the River Dee at several points above and below the old bridge.

Of more local interest is the Llangollen Steam Railway which has been restored by a group of enthusiasts. You can now travel through one of Wales' prettiest valleys in traditional style on one of the restored trains.

Turn right, opposite the 'Bridge End Hotel', cross the road then, within 50 metres, bear left up 'Wharf Hill'. Cross the Llangollen Branch of the Shropshire Union Canal and take the enclosed footpath, up steps, straight ahead; it's signposted to the '*Offa's Dyke Path*'. The path runs uphill beside the local High School. At the top, go through the gate, cross a metalled lane, and continue to climb uphill, through the fields, on a narrow surfaced path beside the hedge. A gate in the top corner leads onto an unmetalled access road— follow this and keep straight ahead at a crossroads by a group of cottages.

At the top of the lane, a gate leads out onto the hillside and a sign to '*Castell Dinas Bran*' directs you half-right. Follow this path over the rise and, after a short dip, a steepening zig-zag path takes you up the neat, sheep-cropped slopes to the crumbling ruins that crown the highest point.

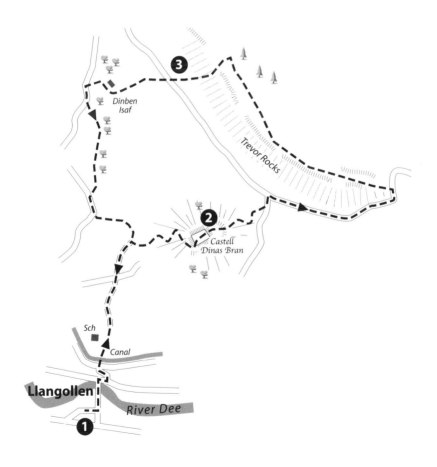

The ruins of castell Dinas Bran

It is hard to picture a more magnificent setting for a castle than this almost fairytale hilltop. Look down from the walls at the tiny figures climbing the steep hillside and you will soon see why the site was chosen. Although today the walls have almost disappeared, enough of the structure remains to form a picture of its original size and layout. Part of a passageway in the wall on the east side and the remains of the Great Hall to the south can still be identified. Outside the walls, a series of earlier Bronze Age earthworks enclose the hilltop.

The origin of the castle is not known for sure but it is thought to have been built to replace an earlier stronghold by Gruffydd ap Madog following his father's death in 1160. As the new Prince of Powys he was only too well aware of the constant threat from across the nearby English border where Norman Marcher Lords waited for their chance to conquer his lands. As a result, he made an alliance with Owain Gwynedd and Rhys ap Gruffydd of Deheubarth.

154

This new threat soon had Henry II gathering his forces and marching west to meet a strong Welsh army assembled at Corwen. For some reason he chose to march over the Berwyn mountains by way of Glyn Ceiriog instead of through the Vale of Llangollen; and it was here that he met with a small force of lightly armed Welsh archers who harassed his army almost killing Henry in one skirmish at Bronygarth below Chirk Castle. These tactics and the appalling weather on the featureless summit of the Berwyns combined to force Henry into a humiliating retreat without even engaging the main Welsh forces. During the retreat Henry took revenge on his captives by tearing out their eyes; among them were the sons of Owain and Rhys.

Despite this victory for the Welsh, Gruffydd decided to pay homage to Henry in 1175 and peace followed until his death in 1191 when his son, Madog ap Gruffydd, replaced him. It was Madog who built the nearby Valle Crucis Abbey in 1201 and reputedly acted as go-between in an important meeting between King John and Llywelyn the Great.

In 1236, he died and was buried at the abbey and succeeded by his son, confusingly called Gruffydd ap Madog. In the unrest that followed Llywelyn's death in 1240 he seems to have been unable to decide where his allegiance lay, although he finally joined Llywelyn II in an ill-fated rebellion with Simon de Montfort, who perished soon afterwards at the Battle of Evesham.

Gruffydd died in 1269 and was followed by his son who died just nine years later—perhaps defending Dinas Bran during one of Edward I's early Welsh campaigns. His two young sons were put into the guardianship of Earl Warren and Earl Mortimer who are said to have drowned them in the River Dee, beneath the arches of the recently completed Holt bridge, in order to take over their lands. Dinas Bran fell for the last time in 1283 during Edward's final crushing of Wales although it continued to have tenants until 1495 when the last owner, Sir William Stanley from Chirk Castle, was executed for his part in a rebellion against Henry VII.

In the following century the castle's only occupant is reported to have been an eagle who fiercely attacked anyone who tried to approach its crumbling walls.

Castell Dinas Bran viewed from Eglwyseg Mountain

2. From the castle ruins, a well marked path descends the eastern slopes of the hill, on the opposite side to the ascent—with a fine view of the Dee valley and Telford's multi-arched aqueduct in the distance—to join a narrow lane below the limestone terraces of Trevor Rocks. Turn left here, then after a few metres turn right at a T junction. This section of road is part of the Offa's Dyke Path (see the OS 1:25,000 Explorer map). Follow the narrow lane gently uphill, as it contours the hillside below the limestone cliffs. When the lane forks, 300 metres later, take the left-hand, upper road.

Five hundred metres or so further on, the lane doglegs sharply around to the left. Immediately before the lane kinks to the right again, turn left, uphill on a broad, signposted path. Follow the path as it rises gently to a gate. Bear left *before* the gate and follow the fenceline diagonally uphill to the edge of the limestone cliffs. The panorama opens up with fine views over the Vale of Llangollen, dominated by Castell Dinas Bran on its conical hill.

Continue along the top of Trevor Rocks past 'Eglwyseg Plantation'—a belt of stunted mature pines angled dramatically away from the prevailing winds.

As the pines peter out, the clifftop path curves to the right, into a V-shaped stream valley cut into the limestone bluffs. At the top of this indentation, a three way wooden fingerpost indicates the way ahead, back, and up to the right. Our route, however, turns sharp left here, to descend through this natural gap in the cliffs. A narrow path runs downhill through the bracken beside a crumbling stone wall and stream. Lower down you are forced to make a short but easy scramble over a low, wet rock step; the driest routes are to either side.

Immediately below the rock step, cross to the right and look for a narrow path *directly below* the sheer rock face. Don't drop too far down the hillside. Once found, the path is clear. It snakes diagonally to the right, downhill through stunted hawthorn and gorse bushes, then crosses screes to the road below. Watch your footing and take care on this section of the route.

3. This attractive lane is part of the Offa's Dyke Path. If you managed to find the correct path down the hillside, directly across the road there should be a field gate and signposted stile. (If, however, you followed the stream down to the road, then turn right and walk up the lane to find the gate and stile just off the road to the left).

Climb the stile and cross the field to the far right-hand corner, ignoring a stile to the left below an old lime kiln. Go through the gate and continue on the farm track ahead, through two more gates. When the track forks, bear to the right, and follow the public right of way through the farmyard to 'Dinbren Isaf' farm. Walk past the old farmhouse with its delightful topiary hedges, and continue down the concrete access drive to a quiet country lane.

Turn left here, downhill, and after about 100 metres, climb over a signposted ladder stile in the hedge on the left. Follow the field edge path downhill beside a wooded stream valley. Watch out for a crude wooden footbridge on the left; cross over and then bear right, gently downhill beneath the trees, with the stream now on your right. Roughly 200 metres later, at a large field gate, bear half-left to a stile to follow an attractive path through open woods, with fields down to the right. At a rough farm track, cross over and go down steps to continue through the trees to a lane. Turn left here, downhill.

When the lane bends to the right, 50 metres later, turn left onto a field path signposted for the '*Llangollen History Trail*'. Keep left around the field edge, with Castell Dinas Bran on its hill now directly ahead. Climb over a stile in the top right hand corner of the field, and then bear right on a shady, uphill path beside the hedge. At the top of the rise, a gate leads back onto the access track used earlier in the walk to reach the castle. Retrace your steps back to Llangollen.

Alternatively, this last section can be avoided by continuing along the lane back to Llangollen to complete the walk.

Other titles from Northern Eye Books:

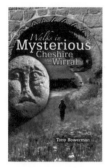

Walks in Mysterious Cheshire and Wirral
Tony Bowerman
ISBN 978 0 9553557 0 7

A new, wholly revised edition of a classic walking book. Fourteen circular walks through Cheshire and Wirral's historic countryside that explore strange and mysterious places along the way. Clear maps and directions. Generously illustrated with rare black and white old postcards and other historic images, and an additional colour section. Paperback. 160 pages.

Walks in West Cheshire and Wirral
Jen Darling
ISBN 978 0 9553557 2 1

A completely new and revised edition of a classic Cheshire walking book. Thirty circular walks in Cheshire and Wirral's 'green and glorious' countryside. Clear maps and directions. Illustrated throughout with black and white photographs, as well as a full colour section. Paperback. 160 pages.

Walking Cheshire's Sandstone Trail
Tony Bowerman
ISBN 978 0 9553557 1 4

The new, definitive walking guide to the Sandstone Trail, a 55 kilometre/34 mile walk from Frodsham to Whitchurch, along Cheshire's beautiful and varied central sandstone ridge. Full colour, illustrated throughout with modern and archive photographs. Route instructions in both directions. Full introduction, interpretation of points of interest, nature notes, places to visit, and accommodation details. Paperback. 224 pages.

To see our full catalogue, visit: **www.northerneyebooks.com**